The Man Who Went to Farr:

Patrick Sellar and the Sutherland Experiment

J. G. LEITH

Baseline Research Ltd

Baseline Research Ltd

ISBN 978-0-9565985-0-9

Printed by Moravian Digital Press, Elgin

To the memory of my parents

Benny Leith, 1918 – 2003

and

Nancy Leith, 1920 – 2008

for instilling the habit of books and reading

Contents

Acknowledgements

My interest in Patrick Sellar goes back many years, having always seen him as something of an enigma. As a result, I have been reading and collecting material throughout this time, which has in some cases made it difficult to be always precise as to where I first read or found it. I have however sought to assign key extracts as accurately as possible, and there is nothing here that is not either in the public domain or available through the many published works, and especially the extensive and informative works of Prof. Eric Richards, without which our knowledge of the Sutherland Clearances would be sadly lacking.

I would like to express my sincere thanks for the assistance and co-operation received from the staff at Staffordshire Record Office, The National Library of Scotland and the National Archives of Scotland.

I have visited and consulted material in various locations, but I would like to make special mention of those in The Highland

Council Archives, Inverness Library, Wick Library and Elgin Library. I should also wish to commend the Strathnaver Museum to anyone interested in the Clearances.

To my daughter Ali, I thank for her careful editing and advice as the manuscript crept nearer to completion.

To Niall Hepburn for his design and photographic skills that have made this more than just words

Above all the support and forbearance I have received from my wife Doreen is immeasurable, without which this would never have reached fruition.

Introduction

The case of Mr Sellar has excited great interest in the North of Scotland, both from the situation
of the gentleman, and from its connection with the new system of management adopted in
Sutherlandshire. Reports were widely spread abroad in regard to Mr Sellar's conduct, and most
erroneous statements given in several newspapers of the whole proceedings.
[Edinburgh Advertiser June 7th 1816]

"There is no quarter of Scotland to which they (Young and Sellar) may retire after having
feathered their nests in Sutherland, but they will pass through life with the halter constantly
about their neck and upon my word, sir, it is but a sorry description of neck cloth."
[Military Register 23rd August 1815]

Patrick Sellar was acquitted, and no one can argue, that in law, he was cleared of all charges brought against him, but just as the Military Register prophesised he was never able to escape the continuing clamour and ever present accusations. At various points throughout his life he felt the need to reiterate his proven innocence and even after his death, his family were moved to continue offering explanations in his defence.

"My father was not a fool or a madman – as such acts if committed would
show him to have been –

but an experienced, able and energetic man of business, who did his duty justly, faithfully and fearlessly, through his whole life." [Thomas Sellar]

Today, the debate rumbles on amidst the ongoing indulgence in discussion about the Highland Clearances. There exists a wealth of published material on the 'clearances', some of which has placed Sellar and his trial in a central position.

But, something, in my opinion, is missing.

The trial of Patrick Sellar was a charade. The verdict may well have been correct according to the law, but the event was stage managed to achieve that verdict.

The witnesses for the prosecution were carefully selected to present a perception of their untrustworthiness and to create confusion around their testimonies. The personal and character witnesses used by Sellar's defence were all 'upstanding' gentlemen and therefore, 'trustworthy'.

There was no desire on the part of the legal authorities to extend this trial to anything more than the day it took to pronounce the verdict, so further examination was never an option.

If we are in any doubt as to whether there was collusion over the whole episode then George MacPherson Grant's note to Lady Stafford in April 1816 may help throw some light on the discussions going on in legal and landowner circles.

> *"I have now to state that I found Mr Gordon of Craig (Senior Counsel for Sellar) here yesterday and that he has given me the most satisfactory account of the result of Sellar's trial the whole of which was calculated to display the arrangements on the Sutherland estate and Sellar's conduct for moderation and humanity in the removal of the people in the most favourable light...The Judge said that although he was not in the habit of making any observations on the verdicts of juries yet he owed it to the character of this much injured gentleman to express his fullest approbation of their verdict on this occasion and the Crown lawyer immediately expressed his concurrence." [Adam]*

William Adam**,** Lord Chief Commissioner of the Scottish Jury Court also put pen to paper within a month of the trial to assure the Staffords that he had had a conversation with the Judge and it all had gone according to plan.

All of this does not make the verdict the wrong one. It does however beg the question - is there a fuller truth? If ALL of those who knew Sellar, and had information on the events in

Strathnaver, had been called to give evidence, would a different picture have emerged?

The aim of this work is to try and create a bigger picture – a picture that still remains incomplete, but may stimulate others who hold missing links and pieces to engage in the debate.

This is the not trial of Patrick Sellar by hindsight but instead a presentation of not just what was examined by the then High Court in Inverness on 26th April 1816, but also what was being said and often inferred by some who never received the opportunity to give evidence and some who were effectively precluded from giving evidence. And yet there were others who knew many of the real truths, but either from fear or for favour remained silent.

Our witnesses all had some knowledge of the events in Strathnaver, some of it maybe not at first hand but they would have been familiar with and close enough in time and place to know where many of the truths lay. In fact this is more an examination of those involved in the Strathnaver Clearances. Patrick Sellar, was acquitted by due legal process, but in truth he was not the only person who might be considered either tainted by the episode or even culpable of creating the means, failing to act or benefiting from the outcomes.

Chapter 1

THE SCENE OF THE CRIME

Patrick Sellar set into motion the removal of families from their homes in Strathnaver in 1814, in accordance with the terms and conditions of the lease he had acquired from the Sutherland Estate, to develop the area as a sheep farm.

Interestingly, Patrick Sellar, the lessee, as Factor on the Sutherland Estate, was also the legal officer responsible for advertising and arranging the lease.

SET OF LANDS AND FISHINGS ON THE ESTATE OF SUTHERLAND

The following parts of the Estate of Sutherland are to be Set, for such number of years as may be agreed on, viz…

V PARISH OF FAR

1. *Kirktomy, Swardly, Fasly and Auchmore*

2. *Rhingvy, Skelpick, Auchinellan and Dunveiden*

3. *Ravigill, Rhiphael, Rheloisk, Rossal, Rhunisdale, and Garvault*

4. *Dalcharrel and Trunderskaig*

5. *Carnachy, and part of the wadsett of Borgie, marching with Invernaver*

6. *Scale and Langdale*

7. *Syre, Kenakyle and part of Grubeg*

8. *Grubeg and Grubmore*

9. *Tubeg, Adraavine of Mudale and Dynachkary*

10. *Bargiebeg*

… persons wishing more particular information may apply to William Young of Inverugie at Rhives or Patrick Sellar in Culmailly, by Golspie.

[Inverness Journal and Northern Advertiser – 16th October 1812]

If anyone showed an interest in the lease, then, Patrick Sellar would have first hand knowledge of any likely bidder and as a consequence, competitor.

The people living in the interior parts of Strathnaver, an area that was now scheduled to become a sheep farm, had through this notice and subsequent pulpit announcements, been notified of their removal and offered new lots of land on the coastal slopes. The above newspaper notice also contained this offer of new land.

Those tenants who may be dispossessed from any of the above farms… will be accommodated on the low grounds, near the sea. [Inverness Journal and Northern Advertiser]

However, come their due time to move, they were still inhabiting the houses and lands that they and their ancestors had occupied over many generations.

Patrick Sellar could wait no longer!

The roof was being demolished and a man with a torch was about to set fire to it.

Hector went up to him. "There's an old bed ridden women in there" he said inoffensively.

"Who told you? Asked the man, with a jeering threat.

"I'm telling you," said Hector, quietly "I'll take her out"

"Who the hell are you?" he shouted, and a man came up whom Hector believed to be Mr Heller, though he had never actually seen him in the flesh before.

"What do you want?" demanded this man in English

Hector had no English and replied in Gaelic.

"He's saying there's an old bed-ridden hag inside," explained the man with the torch.

"Oh is he?" A venomous intensity gathered in the factor's expression. Hector was not an evasive specimen of the native; on the contrary, his large frame and clear-cut features gathered a certain aristocratic antagonism. "Get out of here" said Mr Heller "you lazy devil, clear out!"

Hector gave a pace or two before this explosive violence.

"What about the old woman?" cried the man with the torch, his eyes gleaming.

"Damn her, the old witch, she's lived long enough. Let her burn!" cried Mr Heller

The men, half mad with drink and the growing lust of destruction, gave a laugh. No half-way measures with their factor! Burn the witch!

When the thatch was torn from the roof, fire leapt up. A woman, shouting frenziedly, rushed in at the door.

Hector with his great stride followed her and together, choked and blinded, they groped their way to the aged invalid, picked her up in the bedclothes, and stumbled back through the falling faggots. When he got outside Hector found that the bedclothes were on fire. He laid Morach on the ground and crushed out the fire with his arms and hands, bestriding her in a way that raised a lewd laugh. Her mouth was open, emitting chocking dry sounds as from internal pressure through a pinched wind-pipe. Her eyes rolled. Her whole body heaved, as if the invisible hand were strangling her.

As Morach saw her home in flames, she started crying in a high dolorous voice. Her neck was not strong enough to keep her head steady…. The gaunt witch face behaving in this ludicrous fashion… set the incendiaries into a roar of laughter, not jeering laughter but hilarious mirth. It was the funniest damned thing they'd ever seen! The niceties of respect for the factor's presence had abated. They were all a jovial crew and in it to the neck. Let Factor Heller order: they'd obey to the last. But who said another drink?

Factor Heller was a wise man. This work had to be done; it would, by God, be done thoroughly!

That Gael should curse Gael, that this breed should destroy itself, was necessary for the new order of Progress. Clear them out! Rid the land of such human vermin! For himself and his schemes, he had imported, and would continue to import, thank God, real human beings from the south!

House by house they took them before them, giving the occupants a brief space in which to haul out their belongings, before destroying the dwelling. Pitiful mothers, miserable old men, moaning old women, wailing children, left islanded with their one or two earthly possessions and no home or shelter in the broad world for them. It was a remarkable landscape, acquiring slowly an unearthly demoniac appearance.
[Gunn]

Neil Gunn's account of the burnings is classed as fictional and his ability to use words and language helps create an emotional 'literary' scene. But Neil Gunn knew about this land and its people. It was his land and his people, and the above extract from 'Butcher's Broom' dramatically retells the community memory.

Statements taken from the people of Strathnaver, the 'gloomy memories' of Donald Macleod and evidence provided to the Napier Commission all have the same desperate and anguished ring.

Patrick Sellar's decision to act that day in June 1814 was without doubt catastrophic and momentous for the people of Strathnaver, but little could he have known that it was also to be the catalyst for his own period of Hell.

On 26th April 1816 the Circuit Court in Inverness sat to consider the following indictment:

> *PATRICK SELLAR, now or lately residing at Culmaily, in the parish of Golspie, and shire of Sutherland, and under factor for the Most Noble the Marquis and Marchioness of Stafford. You are indicted and accused, at the instance of Archibald Colquhoun of Killermont, his Majesty's Advocate for his Majesty's interest: That albeit, by the laws of this and of every other well-governed realm, culpable homicide, as also oppression and real injury, more particularly the wickedly and maliciously setting on fire and burning, or causing and procuring to be set on fire and burnt, a great extent of heath and pasture, on which a number of small tenants and other poor persons maintain their cattle, to the great injury and distress of the said persons; the violently turning, or causing and procuring to be turned out of their habitations, a number of the said tenants and other poor people, especially aged, infirm, and impotent persons and pregnant women, and cruelly depriving them of all cover or shelter, to their great distress, and the imminent danger of their lives; the wickedly and maliciously setting on fire, burning, pulling down, and demolishing, or causing and procuring to be set on fire, burnt, pulled down, and demolishing, the dwelling-*

houses, barns, kilns, mills, and other buildings, lawfully occupied by the said persons, whereby they themselves are turned out, without cover or shelter, as aforesaid, and the greater part of their different crops is lost and destroyed, from the want of the usual and necessary accommodation for securing and manufacturing the same; and the wantonly setting on fire, burning, and otherwise destroying, or causing and procuring to be set on fire, burnt, and otherwise destroyed, growing corn, timber, furniture, money, and other effects, the property, or in the lawful possession of the said tenants and other poor persons, are crimes of a heinous nature, and severely punishable. Yet true it is, and of verity, that you the said Patrick Sellar are guilty of the said crimes, or of one or more of them, actor, or art in part; in so far as you the said Patrick Sellar did, on the 15th day of March, 1814, or on one or other of the days of that month, or of April and May immediately following, and on many occasions during the said months of March, April and May, wickedly and maliciously set on fire and burn, or cause and procure John Dryden and John McKay, both at that time shepherds in your service, to set on fire and burn a great extent of heath and pasture, many miles in length and breadth, situate in the heights of the parishes of Farr and Kildonan, in the county of Sutherland, and in particular in the lands of Ravigill, Rhiphail, Rhiloisk, Rossal, Rhimsdale, Garvault, Truderskaig, and Dalcharrel, whereby many of the tenants and others in the lands aforesaid were deprived of pasturage for their cattle, and in consequence thereof reduced to great distress and poverty; and many of them were obliged to feed their cattle with the potatoes intended for the use of their families, and with their seed corn; particularly William Gordon, James McKay, Hugh Grant, and

Donald McKay, all then tenants in Rhiloisk aforesaid ; John Gordon and Hugh MacBeath, then tenants in Rhimsdale aforesaid; Donald MacBeath, then tenant in Rhiphail aforesaid;' Murdo McKay and John McKay, then tenants in Truderskaig aforesaid. And further, you the said Patrick Sellar did, upon the 13th day of June, 1814, or on one or other of the days of that month, or of May immediately preceding, or of July immediately following, together with four or more persons, your assistants, proceed to the district of country above-mentioned, and did, then and there, violently turn, or cause or procure to be turned out of their habitations, a number of the tenants and poor people dwelling there; and particularly Donald McKay, a feeble old man of the age of four-score years or thereby, then residing in Rhiloisk aforesaid; who, upon being so turned out, not being able to travel to the nearest inhabited place, lay for several days and nights thereafter in the woods in the vicinity, without cover or shelter, to his great distress, and to the danger of his life. As also, Barbara McKay, wife of John McKay, then tenant in Ravigill aforesaid, who was at the time pregnant, and was moreover confined to her bed in consequence of being severely hurt and bruised by a fall; and you the said Patrick Sellar did, then and there, notwithstanding the entreaties of the said John McKay, give orders that the said Barbara McKay should be instantly turned out, whatever the consequences might be, saying, That you would have the house pulled about her ears; and the said John McKay was accordingly compelled, with the assistance of some women and neighbours to lift his said wife from her bed, and carry her nearly a mile across the country to the imminent danger of her life: As also, time last above-mentioned, you the said Patrick Sellar did forcibly turn out, or cause and procure your assistants aforesaid, to turn out, of his bed and dwelling, in Gar-vault aforesaid, Donald Munro, a young lad, who lay sick in bed at the time. And further, you the said Patrick Sellar, did time aforesaid, wickedly and maliciously set on fire, burn, pull down, and demolish, or cause and procure your assistants aforesaid to set on fire, burn, pull down, and demolish a great number of the dwelling-houses, barns, kilns, mills, and other buildings, lawfully occupied by the tenants and other inhabitants in the said district of country; and in particular, the houses, barns, kilns, mills, lawfully occupied by the above-mentioned William Gordon, James McKay, Hugh Grant, in Rhiloisk aforesaid; and John Gordon in Rhimsdale aforesaid; As also, the barns and kilns in Rhiphail aforesaid, lawfully occupied by Alexander Manson, John MacKay, and others, then tenants or residenters there; the barns and kilns in Ravigill aforesaid, lawfully occupied by John McKay, Murdo McKay, and others, then tenants there; and the barns and kilns in Garvault aforesaid, lawfully occupied by William Nicol and John Monro, then tenants there; As also, the house and barn in Ravigill aforesaid, lawfully occupied by Barbara McKay, an infirm old widow, nearly fourscore years of age, and who was obliged to sell three of her five cattle at an under value, in order to support herself, her crop being destroyed from the want of her barn : As also, the greater part of the houses, barns, kilns, mills, and other buildings in the whole district of country above mentioned, was, time aforesaid, maliciously set on fire, burnt, pulled down, and demolished, by you, the said Patrick Sellar, or by your assistance or by your orders, whereby the inhabitants and lawful occupiers thereof were turned out, without cover or shelter; and the greater part of their different crops was lost and destroyed from want of the usual and necessary accommodation for securing and manufacturing the same; and especially the lawful occupiers of the barns, kilns, mills, and other buildings particularly above mentioned, to have been set on fire and destroyed as aforesaid, did sustain great loss in their crops, from being thus deprived of the means of securing and manufacturing the same. And further, you, the said Patrick Sellar, did, time aforesaid, culpably kill Donald MacBeath, father to Hugh MacBeath, then tenant in Rhimsdale aforesaid, by unroofing and pulling down, or causing to be unroofed and pulled down, the whole house in Rhimsdale aforesaid, where the said Donald MacBeath was then lying on his sick bed, saving only a small space of roof, to the extent of five or six yards, whereby the said Donald MacBeath was exposed, in a cold and comfortless situation, without cover or shelter, to the weather; and he, the said Donald MacBeath, in consequence of being so exposed, never spoke a word more, but languished and died about eight days thereafter, and was thereby culpably killed by you, the said Patrick Sellar: Or otherwise, you, the said Patrick Sellar, did, time and place aforesaid, cruelly expose the said Donald MacBeath to the weather, without cover or shelter, by pulling down and unroofing, or caused to be pulled down and unroofed, the greater part of the house where he then lay sick in bed, to his great distress, and the imminent danger of his life; and this you, the said Patrick Sellar, did, notwithstanding the entreaties of the said Hugh MacBeath, and others, you saying, in a rage, when it was proposed that the said Donald MacBeath should remain, "The devil a man of them, sick or well, shall be permitted to remain," or words to that effect. And further, you, the said Patrick Sellar, did, time aforesaid, wickedly and maliciously set on fire, burn, and demolish, or cause and procure your assistants to set on fire, burn, and demolish, the dwelling-house, barn, kiln, sheep-cot, and other building then lawfully occupied by William Chisholm in Badinloskin, in the parish of Farr aforesaid, although you knew that Margaret McKay, a very old woman of the age of go years, less or more, and who had been bed-ridden for years, was at that time within the said house ; and this you did, notwithstanding you were told that the said old woman could not be removed without imminent danger to her life ; and the flames having approached the bed whereon the said Margaret McKay lay, she shrieked aloud in Gaelic, "O'n teine," that is to say, "O the fire," or words to that effect; and was forthwith carried out by her daughter, Janet McKay, and placed in a small bothy, and the blanket in which she was wrapped was burnt in several places, and the said Margaret McKay never spoke a word thereafter, but remained insensible from that hour, and died in about five days thereafter, in consequence of the fright and alarm; and, in particular, in consequence of her removal, as aforesaid, from her bed into a cold and uncomfortable place, unfit for the habitation of any human being; and the said Margaret McKay was thereby culpably killed by you, the said Patrick Sellar; or otherwise, you, the said Patrick Sellar, did, time and place aforesaid, cruelly turn, or cause to be turned, out of her bed and dwelling-place, the said Margaret Mackay, by setting on fire, burning, and demolishing, or causing and procuring to be set on fire, burnt, and demolished, the said house and other buildings, in manner above mentioned, to her great distress, and the imminent danger of her life. And farther, all the persons whose houses, barns, kilns, mills, and other buildings, were burnt and destroyed, or caused and procured to be burnt and destroyed by you, the said Patrick Sellar, all as above described, did sustain great loss in their moss wood, and other timber, which was broken and demolished, and destroyed by fire and otherwise, at the same time, and in the same manner, with the buildings as aforesaid; and also in their furniture and other effects, all their lawful property, or in their lawful possession at the time: And, in particular, the said Barbara McKay in Ravigill, aforesaid, lost her door and door-posts, and timber of her house and barn, her meal-chest, and several articles of furniture, all her property, or in her lawful, possession, which were then and there destroyed, or caused to be destroyed, by you, the said Patrick Sellar, as aforesaid ; and the greatest part of the furniture, and timber belonging to the said William Chisholm, together with three pounds in bank notes, and a ridge of growing corn, all the property, or in the lawful possession of the said William Chisholm, in Badinloskin, aforesaid, were then and there destroyed by fire, and otherwise, by you, the said Patrick Sellar. And you, the said Patrick Sellar, having been apprehended and taken before Mr. Robert MacKid, Sheriff-Substitute of Sutherland, did, in his presence, at Dornoch, on the 31st day of May, 1815, emit and subscribe a declaration; which declaration, together with a paper entitled ".Notice given to the Strathnaver tenants, 15 Dec., 1813," being to be used in evidence against you, at your trial, will be lodged in due time in the hands of the Clerk of the Circuit Court of Justiciary, before which you are to be tried, that you may have an opportunity of seeing the same : at least, time and places above-mentioned, the said heath and pasture, was wickedly and maliciously set on fire and burnt, or caused and procured to be set on fire and *burnt, to the great injury and distress of the said tenants and others ; and the said persons were violently turned, or caused and procured to be turned, out of their habitations, and deprived of all cover and shelter, to their great distress, and the imminent danger of their lives; and the said Donald MacBeath and Margaret M` Kay were culpably killed in manner above mentioned, or were cruelly turned out of their habitations as aforesaid ; and the said dwelling-houses, barns, kilns, mills, and other buildings, lawfully inhabited and occupied by the said persons, were maliciously set on fire, burnt, pulled down, and demolished, or were caused and procured to be set on fire, burnt, pulled down, and demolished, and the inhabitants and lawful occupiers thereof turned out as aforesaid; and the greater part of their different crops was lost or destroyed, from want of the usual and necessary accommodation for securing and manufacturing the same; and the growing corn, timber, furniture, money, and other effects, the property, - or in the lawful possession, of the said persons, were wantonly set on fire, burnt, and otherwise destroyed, or caused and procured to be set on fire, burnt, and otherwise destroyed: And you, the said Patrick Sellar, are guilty of the said crimes, or of one or more of them, actor, or art and part. All which, or part thereof, being found proven by the verdict of an assize, before the Lord Justice-General, the Lord Justice-Clerk, and Lords Commissioners of Justiciary, in a Circuit Court of Justiciary to be holden by them, or by any one or more of their number, within the burgh of Inverness, in the month of April, in this present year, 1816, you, the said Patrick Sellar, ought to be punished with the pains of law, to deter others from committing the like crimes in all time coming. [Robertson]*

All of this had been carried out against a people who belonged to and knew no other than what the writer Hugh Miller remembers as an idyllic and peaceable land.

> *"We are old enough to remember the country in its original state, when it was one of the happiest and one of the most exemplary districts in Scotland. It was a country of 'snug farms', the people evenly spread over the interior and the seacoasts living 'in very comfortable circumstances' and in a 'state of trustful security'." [Miller]*

There is a certain irony in that the lifestyle the original inhabitants led and enjoyed, and were being removed from, was pretty close to what their usurpers went on to crave and for many achieve. The lifestyle and the spoils enjoyed from the fishing and shooting estates across the Highlands of Scotland was to become the choice recreation for many of the rich classes. In reality for many of the inhabitants of Strathnaver this idyll was not without hardship, but they bore it with fortitude. Hugh Miller conceded,

> *"Occasional food shortages in the less 'genial' localities commonly in the two months before the crops ripened, but the people always possessed the means and the savings to tide them over such shortfalls." [Miller]*

Angus Mackay was 11 years old during the Strathnaver Clearances that forced him and his family to Strathy Point. Many years later he gave evidence to the Napier Commission:

"I was brought up in Strathnaver and left when I was young and came to Strathy Point when the sheep commenced. If you were going up the strath now you would see on both sides of it the places where the towns were – you would see a mile or half a mile between every town; there were four or five families in each of these towns, and bonnie haughs between the towns and hill pasture for miles as far as they could wish to go. The people had plenty of flocks of goats, sheep, horses and cattle, and they were living happy" [Royal Commission of Inquiry into the Condition of Crofters and Cottars in the Highlands and Islands (Napier Commission)]

Chapter 2

THE SUTHERLAND 'EXPERIMENT'

"In May 1809, Mr Young and I and several other Morayshire men embarked to see this terra incognita. We came into Dunrobin Bay in a beautiful morning, a little after sunrise: and I shall never forget the effect produced upon us by the beauty of the scenery – the mountains, the rocks, wood and the castle reflected on a sea as from a mirror."

Patrick Sellar

A new steam packet service sailing from Burghead in Moray to Golspie in Sutherland was viewed, in Moray and beyond, as an important link to establishing communication networks both north and south. Patrick Sellar, largely through his father's interest, William Young and a group of other Moray men of business established the route and it was on the maiden voyage that Patrick Sellar sailed into Dunrobin Bay and into Sutherland history.

Patrick Sellar entered the world of Sutherland and sheep farming, largely it seems by chance. The Countess of Sutherland's vast estate had long been planning and edging towards sheep farming, but until the arrival from Moray of the new highly charged and ambitious change agents, progress had been slow.

William Young and Patrick Sellar's arrival with ambitious plans and an influx from Lord Stafford's vast fortune, loosened the Countesses improving 'stays' and with her new team she set about turning Sutherland from a largely self sufficient rural economy into a supply house for industrial Britain.

The self-reliance among the people of Sutherland cut no ice with a man of improvement, such as Patrick Sellar.

> *"The people seemed to be all of one profession, that is to say, every man was his own mason, carpenter, tanner, shoemaker…. Every man wore his own cloth, ate his own corn and potatoes, sold a lean kyloe to pay the rent: had no ambition for any comfort or luxury beyond the sloth he then possessed." [Loch]*

The Countess of Sutherland had inherited the Sutherland Estate in 1766 when she was just one year old.

Her father, William Gordon the 17th Earl of Sutherland and his wife both fell ill and died of putrid fever while visiting Bath, leaving Elizabeth to be brought up by her maternal grandmother, Lady Alva.

This was the first time in the long lineage of the House of Sutherland that there was no male heir and it took a considerable legal battle to have Elizabeth's succession confirmed.

Allegations and controversy were hers from the start. Her marriage to George Granville Leveson Gower, one of the richest men in Britain, was claimed to have been mainly for the financial good of the vast, but not very economic, Sutherland Estate.

George Granville Leveson-Gower was the son of the 1st Marquess of Stafford. In turn he became the 2nd Marquess of Stafford, 3rd Earl Gower and Viscount Trentham, 4th Lord Gower of Stittenham in Yorkshire, 8th baronet of the same place on his father's death and ultimately claiming the title of the 1st Duke of Sutherland. George saw Sutherland as a wild, rude county and upon marriage to the Countess set his mind on 'civilising' Sutherland. Money was no object, therefore he was in the easy position to treat it as 'an experiment' In 1807 while touring Sutherland, The Countess and her husband became enthused by the possibility of improvements and as a result Lord Stafford began investing in a coal-pit, salt pans, brick and tile works and herring fisheries, as well, of course, as sheep.

The Countess of Sutherland always remained closely engaged in all decisions regarding the changes on the Sutherland Estate. She employed advisors and factors, she consulted with her husband (after all it was his money she was spending) and she regularly discussed plans and events with her son Earl Gower. Little if anything was done without her knowledge and acquiescence.

The Countesses talents were in fact recognised far and wide and included this accolade from the eminent Swiss social scientist of the time, Simonde de Sismondi (who incidentally was to later become a strong critic of the Sutherland Estate and its management).

> *"The Duchess of Sutherland is, beyond question, an extremely clever woman; she administers her immense fortune with intelligence; she augments it, and for it she prepares fresh enterprises in the future." [Sismondi]*

The Sutherland Estate policies were clearly in line with the Patrick Sellar agenda.

> *"Lord and Lady Stafford were pleased humanely to order the new arrangement of this country. That the interior should be possessed by Cheviot shepherds, and the people brought down to the coast and placed in lots of less than three acres, sufficient for the maintenance of an industrious family, pinched enough to cause them to turn their attention to the fishing.*

A most benevolent action, to put these barbarous Highlanders into a position where they could better associate together, apply themselves to industry, educate their children, and advance in civilisation." [Richards 'Patrick Sellar and the Highland Clearances]]

There is evidence that points towards a bias against the local people ever gaining this opportunity to 'advance in civilisation'. David Stewart of Garth in his weighty, yet often quoted and criticised work on the history of the clans suggested that even the fisheries policy was aimed, wherever possible, at an incoming population.

"Reports are published of the unprecedented increase in the fisheries on the coast of the Highlands, proceeding as it is said from the late improvements; whereas it is well known that the increase is almost entirely occasioned by the resort to fishers from the south. We may turn to an advertisement in the Inverness newspapers, describing sixty lots of land to be let in that country for fishing stations. To this notice is added a declaration that a decided preference will be given to strangers." [Stewart]

The planners employed by the Sutherland Estate submitted their assessment Benjamin Meredith's 1810 report stated,

"The Strathnaver people would benefit from removal and resettlement." [Adam]

Patrick Sellar lost no opportunity to share his views with the Estate on the character of the tenants.

> *"The people are a parcel of beggars with no stock but cunning and laziness Sutherland is a fine country badly stocked. The people have often succeeded against industry – they have wearied out the agents in succession by their craft and their intrigue and combination…They require to be brought to the coast where industry will pay and to be convinced that they must worship industry or starve. The interior of the country is clearly intended by providence to grow wool and mutton for the employment and maintenance and enrichment of industrious people living in the countries suited to manufacture. It is part of the territory of the beasts of the field where it was not meant that man should dwell in cities."* [STAFFORDSHIRE D593]

In case the people of Sutherland were at a loss as to why they were chosen to be players in this great agricultural experiment, James Loch detailed how the officials of the Sutherland Estate explained the plans.

> *"These requirements of the national economy were carefully explained to the ignorant and credulous people of Sutherland and Strathnaver by the factor personally, or by written statements communicated to them by ground officers. That nothing might be omitted in this respect, the different ministers and the*

principal tacksmen within the districts … were written to, explaining to them fully and explicitly the intentions of the proprietors."[Loch]

Certain influences that might suggest and encourage an alternative agenda had to be countered and removed. James Loch again proclaimed a clear route.

"If upon one occasion in the earlier years a momentary feeling of a contrary nature was exhibited, it arose entirely from the misconduct of persons whose duty it was to have recommended and enforced obedience of the laws, in place of infusing into the minds of the people feelings of a contrary description. As soon as the interference of these persons was withdrawn, the poor people returned to their usual state of quietness and repose."[Loch]

Relatively early in his career with the Sutherland Estates, Patrick Sellar saw an opportunity to provide an example for the people of Strathnaver.

"The Strathnaver people are very bad payers and seem totally inactive following the business of eating and drinking more than their farms, and there is much need for some new arrangement among them.
The greater part of the young men of Kildonan have been abroad this last summer at the roads and to the public works and their rents have been paid well." [NLS DEP 313]

Sellar may have been a little premature in praising those of Kildonan, as they were shortly to take exception to their own removal. The Kildonan clearances, however, provided him with an opportunity to demonstrate, albeit from behind a military detachment that he, Patrick Sellar was a force to be reckoned with.[1]

As to the poor people of Rogart, Sellar had no sympathy - but a clear plan.

> *"The people of Rogart which is entirely packed and crammed with whisky smugglers should be cleared to Brora and the straths converted to sheep." [Patrick Sellar]*

And, not only that, these people were Gaels, and to the likes of James Loch, Lord Stafford's Commissioner of Estates, who was an 'experienced' improver and administrator of large estates, their very heritage made them unsuitable and as such should be all but exterminated.

---

[1] The Kildonan Clearances form a crucial part in the history of the Sutherland Clearances, and should be studied as part of gaining a wider understanding of the motives and action of the Sutherland Clearances.

"Gaels were a species of deceit and idleness, by which they contracted the habits and ideas, quite incompatible with the customs of regular society and civilised life." [Loch]

Consequently Loch and other 'civilised' people -

"Would never be satisfied until the Gaelic language and the Gaelic people would be extirpated root and branch from the Sutherland estate." [Mackenzie]

The Strathnaver clearances of course were far from the first. They were merely part of plans that had been laid out much earlier. In 1805 we find the Countess clearly describing the way forward.

"Some people (indeed a good many) must inevitably be tossed out which makes all eyes turn the more to the harbour or at Kilgower and the fishing village. Waste lands that will not do for sheep where we propose to allot for a certain rent a house and an acre to a family, the men will go to work in the south and return to their families in winter, which will introduce industry and bring riches into the country." [NLS DEP 313]

Patrick Sellar's own plans also fitted nicely with the general Estate improvement plans. His feet were barely on dry land after his sea crossing before setting his own agendas in motion with the then Factor, Cosmo Falconer.

'In conversing with Mr Falconer concerning the advantages most likely to arise in Sutherland from the packets we were led to leave an offer with him for one of your Ladyship's farms – Culmailie, measuring about 300 acres. Our offer was one fourth part higher per acre than the rent paid for the same quality of soil by Mr MacKid on the west (Kirkton) and one fifth more than Captain Sutherland on the east (Drummuie) and we could not venture further.' [Patrick Sellar]

The Countess, too, wanted no delay. Her information to Earl Gower suggests that little was going to stand in her way of such a proposal.

"There is a very advantageous offer in the way of improvement for Salloch etc. but which will make it necessary to bribe Sandy Sutherland to give up Culmaily. "I wish you to talk about it to Falconer and see if you can devise any method to get rid of Sutherland." [NLS DEP 313]

Earl Gower and Patrick Sellar seemed at first to find this plan a little harsh. Earl Gower wrote to Sellar saying,

"To deprive Colonel Sutherland of the possession of his house and of the ground he possesses at Culmailly would break his heart." [NLS DEP 313]

Sellar replied,

"We cannot suffer ourselves to be the cause of such an event" [NLS DEP 313]

Nevertheless they proceeded anyway apparently ignoring the poor Colonel.

Between the years 1811 and 1820, 15,000 inhabitants, comprising about 3,000 families became part of the Sutherland Experiment. The outcome of the experiment for these families was a strip of land on the coast that amounted to about two-thirds of an acre for each family. 6,000 acres of 'difficult' land is all they received in return for 794,000 acres of 'good' land for the Sutherland Estate.

Chapter 3

SELLAR'S C.V.

"I fear I have been bred to too much precision and possess too much keenness of temper to be so useful in my office as I ought and sincerely wish to be. A man less anxious might better suit the situation and the nature of the people."

Patrick Sellar

Patrick Sellar was a lawyer by profession and it was for his skills in that capacity that he was initially engaged on the Sutherland Estate. Admittedly, he lost no time in becoming first a very successful, innovative and improving agriculturalist, and then later an equally successful sheep farmer. This success in the world of animals was not to be replicated in his dealings with people.

Sellar was also a very proud man and genuinely considered himself to be a man of high moral character. He was also a vain man and this vanity shows itself when he writes to order his personal seals.

"In case I have not another opportunity of seeing you I send you two seals which have been lying by me uncut and which I will trouble you to get engraved agreeable to the above sketches. The motto which you will not easily read 'veritatem sustine fortiter' (truthfulness to hold up bravely) – the cut intended to

represent a hand holding a pen – this going on the broad one. The other will be
easily comprehended. It goes on the lion's paw." [Fraser]

Sellar never lost an opportunity to do a bit of groveling for the benefit of the Countess, but he made sure that while the tone was suitably obsequious he maintained his own high self opinion.

"I have always been a man with perfect confidence in the good providence that
overrules us and fearless to go where my duty called me. I don't think that I am
blinded by any spiteful voices of self interest; and the more especially I am
satisfied of this that the common sense of what I advocate it so approved that I
cannot think how it comes that everybody does not see it."
[STAFFORDSHIRE D593]

Patrick Sellar had already built up a reputation, not always a positive one, in his hometown of Elgin.

Having studied at Edinburgh University, he then went to work with his father, Thomas, in his Elgin Writer's business. Thomas Sellar was highly regarded by his local land holding clients in and around Moray and Banffshire.

Thomas Sellar was also recognised as providing a solid grounding and training for new entrants into the law businesses.

"The Morayshire proprietors felt the want so much of a good lawyer in Elgin that they sent their Edinburgh agents to send up – one honest lawyer- and Thomas Sellar was selected" – 'Trusty Tom'. [Richards 'The Mind of Patrick Sellar']

Somewhere along the way, Patrick seems to have failed to inherit many of his father's traits. It has been suggested that his early years were lonely ones. His mother died when he was only eight years old and from then on, he was brought up by his father and in a very male dominated environment. Allegedly teased at school on account of his particularly prominent nose, it is maybe no surprise that he early on had to find ways of holding his own in a hostile and critical environment.

"Patrick developed in puberty, not only his great height, but a monstrous nose. For an adolescent loner to contend with school friends ridicule which was impossible to hide, would tend to cultivate a sneering and superior attitude" [Richardson]

While his mother could have had little direct influence on Patrick, she was by all accounts if not a religious zealot, then very devout in her beliefs. His mother's gene pool however may have had some influence on Patrick's propensity to be quarrelsome.

His grandfather. David Plenderleath, an Edinburgh clergyman, had a long-standing and grudge-ridden dispute with his patron The Duke of Buccleuch.

Patrick Sellar did not settle to family life until some two years after his trial. His wife Ann Craig, the second daughter of Thomas Craig of Barmuckity near Elgin was by all accounts a gentle loving and caring wife and mother. She bore him nine children, who in their turn all went on to lead successful and prosperous lives in middle class Victorian style. Ann (Craig) Sellar outlived Patrick Sellar by some years, but continued to refer to him as "my dear Mr Sellar" Despite this adoring and respectful relationship there is no evidence that she changed the nature and approach Patrick Sellar took to those who crossed his paths.

Ann Sellar even welcomed into her family, albeit in a servant capacity, an illegitimate daughter of Patrick's. Jane Sellar or Sutherland, born in 1813, was never denied as the daughter of Patrick Sellar, but she found no place in his final will and testament.

Yet Patrick Sellar came highly recommended by the likes of William Young and George MacPherson Grant, and both must have known that he had the propensity to pick a fight - a reputation that Sellar was not afraid to hide.

Sellar made his employer Lady Stafford aware of his capacity.

> *"I had the Sheriff Clerk of Elgin (a powerful rich man with great interest) suspended from office and made to pay about £500 for partiality two years ago." [Richards 'Patrick Sellar and the Highland Clearances']*

And just in case that failed to get the message across he also informed Lord Gower that –

> *"I have fought some battles against corruption with men of considerable power in Moray." [NLS DEP 313]*

These battles in Moray did not impress some of his combatants.

Patrick Duff, the Sheriff Clerk in Elgin offers a different perspective.

> *"Sellar had some underhand business of his own which leads him to particular inquiries and in order that he might the more easily accomplish his design, called at the Sheriff Clerk's Office on Wednesday 27th May and under pretence at looking for a paper he said had somehow been misplaced got access to transacted processes of the court and ransacked them a whole forenoon from eleven till three*

saying to Patrick Duff on his arrival - "I have mislaid a paper of consequence which I cannot fin; and in case it has been by mistake put into some process am anxious to look over them" – Patrick Duff did not for some time question Mr Sellar's declaration but observing him use a pen and ink which was not necessary in looking for a paper, he began to suspect the declaration and told the Sheriff Substitute, who happened to call that he was not fond of allowing any person to ransack the records in that way." [Fraser]

In 1807, two years before he set foot in Sutherland, Patrick Sellar was being accused of some serious 'double dealing' by James Roy a Heckler in Bishopmill.

"It was the misfortune of the parties to have employed as their agent Patrick Sellar, writer in Elgin, in 1807. To this gentleman, Mr Millar communicated in the most unreserved and confidential manner the state of his affairs and employed him to recover the numerous debts due to him. Sellar was at the same time employed as a man of business by some of Millar's creditors to get payment of the sums due by him; and he made the information that he received in the one capacity completely subservient to his views in the other." [NAS CS38/10/61]

Patrick Sellar and William Young had been closely involved in the project to buy and develop Burghead as a fishing village and port. Here too, Sellar's reputation among the Moray men came under

43

suspicion. Peter Brown of Linkwood, one of the partners in the Burghead project felt somewhat hard done by.

> *"Sellar first bought Burghead and then passed it over to William Young in a somewhat complex and circular set of transactions. Sellar manipulated and connived with Young to deceive and diddle the remaining partners … in order to reap a better price. And thus Young gained Burghead at a bargain price to the disadvantage of the other partners."*

Sellar was forever one to remind people that he was 'in the right'. Letters were written to whoever he thought should listen, telling them plainly that he could never have been in the wrong and usually that the other party was in some way inferior.

In a series of letters to Col. Grant of Grant he sets out his defence while at the same time denigrating the other party. Here again in dispute with Mr Peter Brown of Linkwood in Moray who accused Sellar of some underhand behaviour in terms of the sale of Burghead.

> *"My acquaintance with Mr Brown has not been quite so close as to give probability as to his very extraordinary accusation…. I cannot recollect that I ever embarked my confidence upon him so that it is beyond my skills to devine how he came to be duped by me.*

> *"I decline to do anything further in the matter for the present than just to mention that one sometimes meets in this world with 'boobies' who are come too soon from school and whose folly and impertinence are beneath contempt."*
> [National Archives of Scotland GD248/623/1]

The Countess however was clearly impressed by what William Young had achieved in Moray and saw his skills and ideas as very much in tune with her own.

William Young was a key innovator in the history of land development in Moray. His purchase and improvement of the Inverugie Estate and the subsequent establishment of the fishing village of Hopeman, on the Moray coast, earned him the reputation of being both entrepreneur and improver.

Young's obituary following his death on 20th March 1842 sets out his many achievements.

> *He spent his early and later life in the vicinity of Elgin and for upwards of fifty years had proved a benefactor to the Burgh and County. He was at the head of the movement in the beginning of the century for getting the turnpike roads made in the County, the division of the Aughteen Parte lands of the Burgh, the drainage of the Lochs of Spynie and Cotts, the creation of the harbours of Burghead and Hopeman and the laying of the villages, the*

promotion of the herring fishery, the introduction of steam navigation into the Moray Firth, the gigantic improvements in the County of Sutherland and used every exertion to provide and complete the works of the Caledonain Canal and further the advancement of the North of Scotland. He took a warm interest in young men and procured many situations for those who were deserving, both home and abroad.

Patrick Sellar was one such 'deserving young man'. William Young, described Patrick Sellar's skills to the Countess but also inferred certain limitations might be applied.

"He is quite a bustler and would do remarkably well among the fishermen and kelp makers during the busy season…
"In these places he would be quite in the centre of all and after the farms are laid out he would only have to improve the shores which I believe suits his turn exactly." [Richards 'Patrick Sellar and the Highland Clearances']

Not quite how it turned out and certainly not how Sellar portrayed his own skills and abilities, yet William Young was to be the man in charge and as such he laid out Sellar's job description and duties as 'general manager' –

"His precise responsibilities will be to collect the rents, keep accounts of the expenditure, pay attention to the various rights of the tenants, to their

fulfilment of the conditions of their tacks, to the enforcing of the laws for preserving the plantations and the game, transactions with Ministers and Schoolmasters, framing tacks and other writings." [Adam]

When writing to the Countess in 1815, Sellar saw his role as much more proactive.

"My work is the most arduous operation to drive a stubborn, crafty people against their inclination – that is from idleness to industry." [NLS DEP 313]

Patrick Sellar once he had established himself in Sutherland would be fully at ease criticising his promoter, William Young, but at the stage of gaining acceptance by the Countess he used his association with Young.

"Since I returned to Elgin from my education and joined my father there, I have experienced the greatest friendship from Mr. Young and was more with him than among those of my own years – he would concert and contest and reason points with me as if I was his equal in sense and experience." [Richards 'Patrick Sellar and the Highland Clearances']

The then current Factor to the Countess, Cosmo Falconer offered a note of caution.

" A raw inexperienced young man who could have no claim to the honour your Lordship and family have conferred but from the casual connection with the other (Young) in an adventure in the country in which self-interest as on the other side of the water, stimulates zeal." [NLS DEP 313]

William Mackenzie, the Countesses Edinburgh lawyer was not likely to offer Sellar a testimony.

"Where ever taste, temper or feeling is required or even ordinary discretion he (Sellar) is deficient beyond what I ever met in any man, so that I don't know one in the whole circle of my acquaintance so ill calculated to fill the office of a factor and in such a county as Sutherland." [Adam]

The Countess however, at first, found Sellar's work to be unimpeachable.

"Following a tete a tete with Sellar this morning and I have read his rentals – all perfection like Bradshaw's, and as neat."[Richards 'Leviathan of Wealth']

His agricultural achievements also met with approval from the Countess.

"I visited Sellar's farm at Culmaily – he is busy making hay and is to have it in a large

hayrick in a fortnight. We see his farm in excellent order. He has taken in 24 acres of the large green nobby field above his house, the taking four large stones out cost £80. He does the other half next year. He made £500 profit last year of his cattle. The sheep we are to hear of as we had not time to go back to see the wool. The black houses are levelled, making manure. The plain is really a very fine sight."[Adam]

James Loch too, was at first, impressed.

> *"Sellar is a man of sharpness and accuracy who will make people pay and also enforce the law strictly. I have been bit by Sellar and am possessed with the same love of penmanship." [Adam]*

It didn't take Sellar too long however to start to show his true colours and jettison his 'great friend', William Young. The Countess in 1811 noted,

> *"Sellar has no sense and perhaps we may be as well without him; it is quite ridiculous that from a jealousy which I see he entertains of Young's nephew that he should go on in this manner" "Young is the important person, the other is nothing without him altogether" "Sellar is a clever writer and accountant and very zealous, but I think perhaps at times too much so without direction." [NLS DEP 313]*

The jealousy was maybe not all one-way however. William MacKenzie, the Countesses, Edinburgh lawyer observed,

> *"I do believe he (William Young) has more than a jealousy of Sellar, he dislikes the manner of his occasional interference."* [NLS DEP 313]

Young did suggest that Sellar might eventually take over from him.

The Countess was not convinced of the idea.

> *"Sellar I am convinced would not do well and without raising eternal riots and complaints."* [NLS DEP 313]

Sellar was also of course quick to point out that his ideals were conversant with that of his employer.

> *"I was at once a convert to the principle now almost universally acted on in the Highlands of Scotland, viz that the people should be employed in securing natural riches of the sea coast …"* [Richards 'Patrick Sellar and the Highland Clearances']

This sits somewhat uncomfortably with an earlier statement attributed to Patrick Sellar.

"I was filled with the belief that the growth of wool and sheep in the Highlands was one of the most abominable and detestable things possible to be imagined and that inroads then making on the ancient habits and manners of the children of the Gael were cruel and extreme" [Richards 'Patrick Sellar and the Highland Clearances']

In truth Sellar had little sympathy or compassion for the children of the Gael.

> *"I believe that Gaelic is a dying language and impeding progress in the Highlands. I would therefore suppress the reading of Gaelic and induce the study of English as much as possible."* [NLS DEP 313]

To complete his obsequiousness and prove his understanding of the people he played the 'common man' card.

> *"My great grandfather was a small tenant removed from a let poor place like Rhimsdale in the heights of Banffshire. The honest man was no doubt cruelly used – he was forced to apply to industry and to put his sons to business in place of keeping them idly about him. But what do I not owe the proprietor that he had the humanity to drive us to our thrift. I am not superstitious but I believe in my heart that it is out of the great goodness of providence that he put it into the minds of such great people as Lord and Lady Stafford and your Lordship to force us to what is proper for us and for the general welfare of every creature unto you."* [NLS DEP 313]

But the sheen was beginning to wear off. The Countess began to review her earlier comments.

> *"Sellar is an excellent man of business but has not enlarged views, and plagues people with trifles."* [Richards 'Patrick Sellar and the Highland Clearances']

Patrick Sellar, whatever else he was or did, was a forward thinking and innovative agriculturalist.

His crop management along with his sheep farming methods were recognised at the time. George Tollet, himself an eminent agriculturalist was full of praise.

> *"Mr Sellar is in my estimation one of the best agriculturalists in the Empire and an honour to his country. Sutherland, I hope in all time coming will feel the benefit of his successful labours." [NLS DEP 313]*

Chapter 4

LET BATTLE COMMENCE

*Mr Patrick Sellar at Culmaily, Factor to the Marchioness and Marquis of Stafford –
Incarcerated by warrant of Robert MacKid, Esq. Sheriff Substitute of Sutherland. On a charge
of having wilfully set fire to a house of a tinker in Badiloskin of Rossal in Strathnaver and
demolishing the mill of Rhimsdale, both part of Mr Sellar's own sheepfarm. Committed to jail
betwixt the hours of 5 and 6 in the morning.*

The Dornoch Jail entry 31ˢᵗ May 1815

Patrick Sellar knew the law. He was experienced in the application
of it and was no stranger to using it for self and client interest.
Maybe it was because of this close knowledge of how the law could
be worked that he was genuinely terrified when it was about to be
used against him.

> *"The petitioners against me are a few tools employed for a purpose. Mr
> Cranstoun will settle it and your Ladyship will in time comprehend their story
> better than you can possibly do at present." [NLS DEP 313]*

But Mr Cranstoun didn't 'settle it' and Patrick Sellar found himself
in Dornoch Jail and desperately writing to the Countess.

> *"Little did I think when I last had the honour to address your Ladyship that my
> next letter should be from Dornoch prison. My Lord Gower is so good as to say*

on the Strathnaver peoples petition 'that proper steps be taken for laying the business before the Sheriff Depute that a full hearing may be given to all parties the petitioners will therefore be assisted by him if they desire in it having a precognition taken before him' Instead of which Mr MacKid my personal enemy takes a partial case from the complainers which I doubt not he has inflamed with all the art in his power and he has straightway committed me to prison without allowing me to speak or to see the face of a magistrate His hope is to concuss me to ruin my character by clamour and to derange my affairs...I formerly mentioned to your Ladyship the powerful opposition I had in Leith's case and the inference I drew I beg to remind your Ladyship of the papers I sent you in 1811 on this business. Perhaps you will be so kind as send them to me in course of post as they are material for my case. (Robert Leith, tenant of Culgower claimed to hold a lease of the east coast kelp from Hugh Houston, tacksman. Sellar attempted to restrict his operations and Leith brought an unsuccessful action against him in the Court of Session for damages. Cosmo Falconer acted as Leith's agent and Sellar suspected that William Mackenzie was a party to this.)" [Adam]

Robert MacKid lost no time in informing Lord Stafford that he the Sheriff Substitute was about to rid his lordship and the Sutherland Estate of an evil presence.

"I conceive it a duty I owe to your Lordship to address you upon the present occasion and a more distressing task I have seldom had to perform.

54

Your Lordship knows that in the summer last a humble petition subscribed by a number of tenants on Mr Sellar's sheep farm in Farr and Kildonan was presented to Lady Stafford complaining of various acts of injury, cruelty and oppression alleged to have been committed upon their persons and property by Mr Sellar in the spring and summer of that year. To this complaint her ladyship upon the 22nd of July last was graciously pleased to return an answer in writing. In it her Ladyship with her usual candour and justice with much propriety observes – That if any person on the estate shall receive any illegal treatment she will never consider it as hostile to her if they have recourse to legal redress as a most secure way to receive the justice which she always desires they should have on every occasion. Her Ladyship also intimates – that she had communicated the complaint to Mr Sellar that he may make proper enquiry and answer to her. It would appear however that Mr Sellar still refused or delayed to afford that redress to the removed tenants to which they conceived themselves entitled, which emboldened them to approach Lord Gower with a complaint, similar to the one presented to her Ladyship. To this complaint his Lordship graciously condescended under date 8th February last to return such an answer as might have been expected from his Lordship. His Lordship says that he has communicated the contents to your Lordship and Lady Stafford who as his Lordship nobly expresses himself – are desirous that the tenants should know that It is always their wish that justice should be impartially administered. His Lordship then adds, that he has sent the petition with directions to Mr Young that proper steps should be taken for laying the business before the sheriff depute and that the petitioners would therefore be assisted by Mr Young if they desired *it in having the precognition taken before the sheriff-depute according to the petition. Soon after receipt of Lord Gower's letter it would appear that a copy of the petition with his Lordship's answer had been transmitted to the sheriff depute by the tenants. `Mr Cranstoun in answer upon 30th March last says that if the tenants mean to take a precognition immediately it will proceed before the sheriff substitute as my engagement will not permit me to be in Sutherland until the month of July. In consequence of these proceedings on an express injunction from his Majesty's advocate depute and a similar one from the sheriff depute I was compelled to enter upon an investigation of the complaints. With this view I was induced to go into Strathnaver where at considerable personal inconvenience and expense and with much patient perseverance I examined about forty evidences upon the allegations stated in the tenants petition; and it is with the deepest regret I have to inform your lordship that a more numerous catalogue of crimes, perpetrated by an individual has seldom disgraced any country or sullied the pages of a precognition in Scotland. This being the case the laws of the country imperiously call upon me to order Mr Sellar to be arrested and incarcerated in order for trial and before this reaches our Lordship this preparatory legal step must be put in execution. No person can more seriously regret the cause nor more feelingly lament the effect than I do; but your Lordship knows well and as Earl Gower very properly observed – justice should be impartially administered. I have in confidence stated verbally to Mr Young my fears upon this distressing subject and I now take the liberty of stating my sentiments also to your lordship in confidence." [Robertson]*

The situation was quickly communicated to William MacKenzie, the Countesses Edinburgh lawyer. He informed the Advocate Depute of MacKid's position.

> *"His opinion in point of law is that Sellar is not guilty of wilful fire-raising but is guilty of culpable homicide and criminal oppression and that a trial must take place. He repeated to me that he considered Sellar's conduct as extremely cruel and oppressive."* [NLS DEP 313]

The Military Register which had anticipated the finding's in MacKid's precognition with remarkable accuracy, put it's own spin on events.

> *"The sheriff (MacKid) was so affected by the detail that he fainted in the corner overpowered by his own feelings."* [Richards 'Military Register and the Pursuit of Patrick Sellar']

William Young, ostensibly Sellar's boss, hated conflict and disagreement and indeed was accused of having "fled south at the time of MacKid's precognition to avoid interrogation".

Young was a man that wished for speedy conclusions that generated as little fall out as possible.

"I was really in hopes that all this jarring had been amicably adjusted betwixt Mr Sellar and the tenants and that the noble family would never have heard more of it. I wish there is not some incendiary at the bottom of it however the truth will come out and it is right is should." [Adam]

Robert MacKid the arresting officer however can have done little to assuage Young's hopes of a quiet and satisfactory conclusion. Following the meeting with MacKid, Young observed,

"With a demure face he told me that Sellar must be hanged or at any rate sent to Botany Bay and he advised me to have no communication with him." [NLS DEP 313]

The Sutherland Estate did not wish to be seen as directly taking sides. After all, the accusers were the Marchionesses 'people' and she must be seen to be the caring and benevolent landlord.

"The family would not screen a servant from prosecution nor regard legal proceedings as hostile to them." [Richards 'Military Register and the Pursuit of Patrick Sellar']

On the other hand, Patrick Sellar was her employee and acting at least in part in accordance with her plans.

"Sellar should get all the proper assistance and protection we can give him. We must be very firm not to give way in this affair or that would put an end to all things." *[STAFFORDSHIRE D593]*

James Loch the Stafford's chief commissioner shared the thinking with his uncle, Chief Commissioner of the Jury Court in Scotland.

"The Staffords had a high opinion of Sellar's honesty and zeal for their service and interest and the management of the affairs under his charge. Of his discretion and temper in putting the people out and whether he may have been too hasty in some of his acts is a different question… there is no wish to screen him." *[Richards 'Patrick Sellar and the Highland Clearances']*

Sellar then set about contesting not just the evidence but also the process itself. He sought to convince James Loch of the travesty of the legal process being applied.

"None of the precognition evidence was taken under oath. MacKid knew well they could not swear to what he took down from them He misled to kill me by defamations not by law." *[Richards 'Patrick Sellar and the Highland Clearances']*

Moves were instigated to settle the matter without recourse to the law courts. The Rev David Mackenzie was asked to arbitrate.

"I received a letter from Mr Campbell, the Crown Agent for Scotland, proposing a submission – that is to say a legal agreement over damages, which would obviate the need for a criminal trial. The complainants refused this course of action, as they understood that they had been promised a full criminal trial of Sellar." [Paton]

William Grant of Rhives informed the Factor, William Young, of the tenants continued determination.

"John Munro deputed by the rest of Mr Sellar's friends in Strathnaver has just now called to say that they unanimously agree to adopt a legal procedure against Mr Sellar rather than to enter into a submission, as he insinuated that as Mr Sellar had dealt with them so harshly they now wish the case to be made as public as possible... I understood that they had been consulting with some person of the law." [Adam]

The said John Munro a tenant in Strathnaver, duly wrote to the Advocate Depute.

"There are many instances of grievous oppression by which I and a great many of my poor neighbours and acquaintances have suffered severely. A number of poor illiterate tenants as we are could have but a small chance of success in this manner against one who is himself a Lawyer [that is Patrick Sellar] who has so much power and that power is derived from the Marquis and Marchioness of

Stafford, unless some independent person of ability and interest would befriend us and take an interest in our case." [NLS DEP 3134]

The force of the legal establishment in Scotland was brought to bear and Patrick Sellar, released from his prison, retired to his home in Elgin to prepare his defence - further proof that he was taking this seriously and knew the potential consequences.

Sellar compiled copious notes and briefings and argued points of law as to the documents he should be allowed to see in advance of his trial. It is doubtful, given the way the trial proceeded and the conduct of those charged with carrying out the process of law, that Sellar needed this extent of preparation.

Despite all the discussions, pleadings and processes, Patrick Sellar was finally brought to trial in Inverness.

"Patrick Sellar now or lately residing at Culmaily in the parish of Golspy and Shire of Sutherland and Under Factor for the most noble The Marquis and Marchioness of Stafford is indicted and accused at the instance of His Majesty's Advocate for His Majesty's Interest of the crimes of culpable homicide and oppression as particularly mentioned in the Indictment raised and pursued against him. The libel being read over to the Pannel in open court and he being interrogated thereupon pleaded Not Guilty." [Robertson]

The following were all solemnly sworn in as the Jury:

James Fraser of Belladrum

William Fraser of Culbockie

William Mackintosh of Balnespick

Duncan Fraser of Fingask

Alexander Smith, merchant in Inverness

John Gillanders of Highfield

William Reid of Muirtown

William Mackenzie of Strathgarve

George Falconer MacKenzie of Allangrange

Robert Denham, tacksman of Dunglass

George Kay, residing at Tannachy

Bailie Robert Ross, merchant in Elgin

John Barclay, writer in Elgin

John Collie, farmer in Alvas

John Smith, tacksman of Greens

The Prosecution then rose and called Robert MacKid, Sheriff Substitute of Sutherlandshire.

Immediately, the Defence objected to McKid's evidence on a range of points that included his personal 'malice' towards the defendant and on claims that as Sheriff-Substitute he had failed in the various legal procedures of imprisonment. MacKid was further accused of sending an "inflammatory and false statement of the pretended circumstances of the case to the Marquis of Stafford". The final objection was that Robert MacKid had stated to various persons that Sellar should "be hanged and that Botany Bay was too good for him."

The Court allowed the objections and MacKid was effectively silenced.

The Prosecution proceeded to call a number of Strathnaver tenants. Some of them spoke little or no English and through cross-examination were generally made to contradict each other in regards to details. Other potential witnesses were rejected on the basis that they had been "erroneously described". Mr Robertson, for the Defence called for the following defences to be read:

"First, The panel objects to the relevancy of various parts of the libel. Second, In so far as the libel is relevant, the panel denies its truth; the whole of the charges are utterly false, in so much so, that the Prosecutor is not only unable to bring any sufficient evidence in support of his own accusations, but the panel will bring positive proof against them. The panel will prove, that the ejectments which have given rise to this trial, were done in due order of law, and, under the warrants of the proper Judge, issued on regular process. Farther, he will prove that great indulgence was shown to the tenants, even after they had resisted the regular decrees of the Judge; that nothing was done on his part, or with his knowledge or approval, cruel, oppressive or illegal. That he committed no acts of homicide; and, on the whole, he will prove, that throughout every part of this affair, he (the panel) has been the victim, not only of the most unfounded local prejudices, but of long continued and active defamation, on the part of certain persons, who have made it their business to traduce the whole system of improvements introduced into the Sutherland estate, and to vilify the panel, by whom, they have been pleased to suppose, that these improvements have been partly conducted. He rejoices, however, in the first opportunity, which has now been afforded to him, of meeting these calumnies and prepossessions in a Court of Justice, and relying, as he does, with implicit confidence on the candour and dispassionate attention of a British jury, he has no doubt whatever of being able to establish his complete innocence of all the charges now brought against him. He gave a short sketch of the causes which gave rise to the present trial, — alluded to the clamour which had been raised in the country—the prejudices of

the people, —the disgraceful publications in a newspaper called the Military Register, and the pains which had been taken to circulate these false and mischievous papers through Sutherland and the adjacent counties. The general line of defence he stated to be, That, as to the first charge, of heath-burning, this was done with the express consent of the tenantry, and, as could be proved, to their positive advantage. As to the removings, the defence was quite clear. The lands mentioned in the indictment were advertised to be set on the 5th of December 1813, at the Inn of Golspie, and Mr. Sellar was preferred as the highest offerer. Before Whitsunday, 1814, he brought regular actions of removing, and it was not until after he had obtained decrees in these actions, charged the whole of the tenants to remove, and taken out precepts of ejection against them, that they were, in the month of June, actually removed from their lawless and violent possession. These facts were established by the decrees and precepts in the hands of the Clerk of Court. As to the demolition of the houses, no houses were pulled down till after the ejections had been completed, and the property had become Mr. Sellar's. No furniture was destroyed by him, or by his orders, —no unnecessary violence was used, nor any cruelty exercised, but everything was done in due order of law, and without oppression of any kind. The charges of culpable homicide were quite out of the question, and Mr. Sellar defied the Public Prosecutor to prove them. Upon the whole, it was not doubted, that if truth and justice were to prevail over malice and conspiracy, Mr. Sellar would obtain an honorable and triumphant acquittal." [Robertson]

Sellar's Counsel, Lord Cockburn put up a stout defence of his client.

> *"My client has been shamefully persecuted and whatever the result may be he is innocent as innocence itself. His only risk arises from the gross local prejudices which have been indulged against him for two years and which it is difficult for even an honest jury to get out of their heads." [NLS DEP 313]*

One witness listed by the defence was Donald MacLeod, a stonemason from Strathnaver. Interestingly he was never called to give evidence in support of the defendant, yet he was by his own admission an eyewitness.

It remains something of a mystery as to why he was listed as a defence witness, if what he was later to publish in his 'Gloomy Memories', was indeed his eyewitness account.

> *"I was an eyewitness of the scene… Strong parties furnished with faggots and other combustibles rushed on the dwellings… and immediately commenced setting fire to them… The consternation and confusion were extreme. The cries of the women and children, the roaring of the affrighted cattle hunted by the yelping dogs of the shepherds amid the smoke and fire… presented a scene that completely baffles description." [MacLeod 'Gloomy Memories']*

Donald Macleod's versions of events have been called into some question both in terms of their complete veracity and because of his desire to castigate both the Sutherland family and Rev. David Mackenzie for the alleged mistreatment of him and his family.

Other witnesses were called to contradict the evidence of the tenants and to show that all removings were carried out according to law and custom.

The defence finally introduced a number of character witnesses, whom the Judge was later to invite the Jury to compare the stature of such gentlemen to that of the tinker and other prosecution witnesses in terms of likely trustworthiness.

Brodie of Brodie

"Sellar was a person of the strictest integrity and humanity, incapable of being even an accessory to any cruel or oppressive action."

Sir George Abercromby of Birkenbog

"I have always thought him a young man of great humanity, and I think him incapable of being guilty of the charges… and trust, upon trial, they will turn out to be unfounded, and put a stop to this clamour which is so disagreeable."

That George Abercromby would have known Patrick Sellar is not in any doubt as he held the position of Sheriff of Elgin from 1783 to his death in 1831. In this capacity he would have encountered Sellar on a fairly regular basis – Patrick Sellar being for a time Procurator Fiscal for Moray.

Abercromby's standing as a character witness would have impressed any jury of the time. Born into the Baronetcy of Birkenbog, near Cullen, in 1750, he became an Advocate in 1773 and then ten years later beginning his term of Sheriff of Elgin. Also in 1783 he married Jean Ogilvy, daughter and heiress of Lord Banff and in this capacity she inherited the estate of Forglen in Banffshire in 1803.

Sheriff Substitute of Elgin and Nairn

" I have always known him to be a man of sympathy, feeling and humanity."

Sheriff-Substitute of Inverness

"He has known the panel from his boyhood. He has borne a most respectable character and is known to the witness to be of a humane disposition [and] conceives him incapable of doing anything cruel or oppressive."

Sir Archibald Dunbar of Northfield *presented the same statement as the above Sheriff Substitute.*

The trial now took something of an unusual turn. The prosecution had already decided not to call all of its witnesses, as it did not want to waste the Court's time in simply repeating what already had been heard. The Advocate-Depute declared

> *"That he thought it fair to the panel, and that it would be satisfactory to the jury, to state his conviction, that if those witnesses who were rejected on account of errors in their designations, had been examined, the result of the trial would have been the same." [Robertson]*

Crown then addressed the jury and stated that:

> *"He gave up all the charges except the one which regarded the ejections from the barns, and that of real injury in the case of the old woman at Badinloskin. He certainly did not think the evidence in this case last was sufficient to establish culpable homicide; but he argued, that the circumstances proved were sufficient to authorise the jury in finding a verdict of guilty to the extent of an injury, as she had been removed at the risk of her life, which he maintained to be contrary to law. As to the barns, he contended that the conduct of Mr. Sellar was irregular and illegal, and consequently oppressive, the outgoing tenants being entitled, by the custom of Sutherland, to retain them as long as the arable land." [Robertson]*

Summing up for the defence Mr Gordon,

"...entered at great length into the history and objects of the prosecution; the preconcerted plan on which certain persons had instigated the people of Strathnaver to complain at first, and to persist afterwards; the views they entertained of successfully opposing the improvements of Sutherland, by affecting the noble persons to whom the property belonged, through the sides of Mr. Sellar, as a convenient medium of succeeding; the disgraceful measures to which these persons had resorted, with a view to affect the channels of justice, the impartiality of jurymen, and the purity of evidence. He attacked the measures and conduct of Mr. MacKid in the most pointed terms; exposed the characters of the evidence of Chisholm and others, and dwelt in the clear evidence of the total innocence of Mr. Sellar, and on the points of law which applied to the particular charges as criminal charges, at considerable length, and with reference to various law authorities; and finally, concluded by maintaining to the jury, that this was not merely the trial of Mr. Sellar, but, in truth, a conflict between the law of the land and a resistance to that law: That the question at issue involved the future fate and progress of agricultural, and even moral improvements, in the county of Sutherland; that (though certainly not so intended by the Public Prosecutor, whose conduct throughout has been candid, correct, and liberal), it was nevertheless, in substance, and in fact, a trial of strength between the abettors of anarchy and misrule, and the magistracy, as well as the laws of this country." [Robertson]

Judge Pitmilly also sought to help the Jury on the character of the accused.

> *" If the jury were at a loss .... They ought to take into view the character of the accused; for this was always of importance in balancing contradictory testimony... and must have some weight with the jury." [Robertson]*

The jury retired for a quarter of an hour, returned and delivered a verdict, unanimously finding Mr. Sellar NOT GUILTY.

Lord Pitmilly, endorsed their decision as he observed that,

> *"...his opinion completely concurred with that of the jury." [Robertson]*

In dismissing the Jury and sympathizing with them about so long a trial, he was happy to say,

> *"They had paid the most patient attention to the case, and had returned a verdict satisfactory to the Court." [Robertson]*

And, just so no one was in any doubt, Judge Pitmilly concluded by saying-

> *"He owed it to justice to declare, in this particular case, that the verdict met with his full perfect concurrence... It appeared quite evident that the whole of this case originated in misconception, malice and personal hostility. Sellar had been the victim of instigators...in the background who had incited the deluded people to resistance and misrepresentation. Sellar was praised for his*

moderation, kindness of disposition and his love of the sick and the infirm…even in the very circumstances complained of, very cautious and remarkable." [Robertson]

Lord Pitmilly finally addressed Patrick Sellar.

"Mr. Sellar, it is now my duty to dismiss you from the bar; and you have the satisfaction of thinking, that you are discharged by the unanimous opinion of the jury and the Court.

I am sure that, although your feelings must have been agitated, you cannot regret that this trial took place, and I am hopeful it will have due effect on the minds of the country, which have been so much, and so improperly agitated." [Roberstson]

The trial lasted from ten o'clock on Tuesday through to one o'clock on Wednesday morning As evidence of just how much Sellar was concerned about the trial comes from the Lady Stafford's confidential court respondent.

"It lasted 14 hours. Sellar bore up very well but when the verdict was pronounced he burst into tears which had a great effect on the audience." [NLS DEP 313]

Lady Stafford took a more dispassionate view.

72

"The trial had been of service in putting down that whole opposition"
[Richards 'Patrick Sellar and the Highland Clearances']

The now disgraced Sheriff Substitute, Robert MacKid was later to state what many have felt both then and since.

"The proof afterwards fell short and that the prisoner was acquitted is perfectly true, but this circumstance can infer no damages against a magistrate who acted bone fide and the result of a precognition impartially taken. Moreover, when it is said that the pursuer was acquitted, it ought to be stated that it was not upon a full hearing of the evidence examined in the precognition, but after the rejection of seven material witnesses out of the small number precognised who had been brought forward to be examined [National Archives of Scotland CS 232/S23/2]

This is further corroborated in Donald Macleod's 'Gloomy Memories', himself a defence witness although not called to give evidence.

"Of the forty witnesses examined at the precognition before the sheriff there were only eleven … were brought forward for the crown."

Chapter 5

UPON REFLECTION

"The Chronicle's campaign is to stir up the unwashed part of mankind against those who shave and wear a clean shirt"

Patrick Sellar

Patrick Sellar was no shrinking violet when it came to proclaiming his opinion or triumphing in his own or his family's success. His trial however brought him and his employers into a public light that they would not have chosen. Patrick Sellar, from that day on, was forced to defend himself and his actions.

"I am the first man brought to trial for having under the sheriff's warrant turned out a tenantry, violently retaining possession, a month after the ground had been advertised, five months after it had been publicly set to another, three months after they had got notice to quit and one month after it had become the property of the new tenant whose payment for it had begun and thus ceased to exist. I feel astonishment how it is credible that I a man originally of some humble independence and prospects in life to which was added the honour of Lord Stafford and your Ladyship's confidence should without any imputation of insanity, of private interest, of malice, of passion, go furth in broad day in prescience of officers and witnesses to commit crimes!

74

I feel confident of acquittal, notwithstanding the perjury to be expected of highland witnesses – the bias of a highland jury and the circumstances that Lord Pitmilly who is to be my judge is brother of the partner of Mr MacKenzie whose influence I believe did at the first foster and bring forward this and similar oppressions against me. I trust the last circumstance is accidental and I rely on the paternal care of providence who watches over all, guides all human events and in the wisdom and goodness of whose decrees I entertain full and implicit confidence." [NLS DEP 313]

Despite this 'full confidence' Sellar had been terrified by the whole experience. Writing to James Loch, he expanded on this genuine fear.

"If you had been as nearly hanged as I had was by Highland cunning and knew, as I do, how perfectly harmless and within the permission given my conduct has been and had made the same discoveries when I have done, in other things, you would feel as I do vigilant against such practices." [STAFFORDSHIRE D593/K/1/316]

Throughout the rest of his life, Patrick Sellar was to confidently, if somewhat wearily face and confront direct attacks.

"During the whole struggle from 1810 downwards I have done without flinching and without fear what I thought incumbent on me to the best of my knowledge and I will not fall back in these latter days taking care however to act

in so important an affair with the best advice and so as best to promote the cause of order, truth and justice." [Patrick Sellar]

But he retained a fear of what was liable to come up behind him.

"I have no fear of death by the hand of any man who will look me in the eye; but I am not less liable to assassination." [NLS DEP 313]

Patrick Sellar, maybe rightly, saw conspiracy at every turn but he was determined to have revenge.

"The people have insinuated and sneaked and whispered calumnies against me. The people are led from above and it is now imperative to find out and punish the leaders of the people." [Richards 'Patrick Sellar and the Highland Clearances']

He knew who the enemies were.

"I shall make a point of having MacKid well trounced." [NLS DEP 313]

"The Sutherlands and MacKid were the ostensible leaders in the plot designed to force or intimidate us to a trial of me." [Richards 'Military Register and the Pursuit of Patrick Sellar']

His archenemy Robert MacKid may have had some foresight into the fact that the press would not let the matter lie when, as part of his written apology, MacKid had requested Sellar not to publish it in the newspapers.

> *"I beg further to add that in case of your compliance with my wish here expressed you are to be at liberty to make any use you please of this letter, except publishing in the newspapers which I doubt not you will see the propriety of my objecting to."*

Maybe Sellar hoped that others would 'publish' it for we know he sent copies to at least the Duke of Sutherland and James Loch, while seeking to defend himself against the newspapers. In an 1841 letter to James Loch, Sellar makes it clear that they may want to refer to it.

> *"You will be surprised to see me trouble you with the enclosed copies of my statement concerning McKid's conspiracy of the years 1814 -15 & 16 and to learn that I have sent other two copies to his Grace in case reference to such should be wanted at this time.*
> *"A radical paper in Edinburgh, I mean a regular 'movement' paper, that excited the mob against the powers that be, is (and has been for some weeks) carrying on an attack against the Sutherland Family in an article headed 'Destitution in Sutherland' and therein it has found it important to reassert as truth all that the Jury found to be a fiction and all that MacKid himself acknowledged in the enclosed 'to amount to absolute falsehoods'.*

"One would say that in the circumstances such an affair as this is beneath contempt and so it in truth and in sober minds is; but still in these times it calls for cool reflection."

Patrick Sellar was not of course content to leave it to chance that the press might just go away upon 'cool reflection'.

"I have written to Walter Horsburgh W S who does my little business in Edinburgh, requesting him to take for me the advice of Counsel what I ought to do and what it may be in my power to do; and I will be very much obliged to you to give me the benefit of your clear judgement on the same subject. I want to do (as I always have studied to do) my duty well and thoroughly without asking whether that duty be pleasant or not. I should think that it may be in my power to put these noises to silence and to punishment too without reference to any questions as betwixt them and the Noble Family." [STAFFORDSHIRE D593/P122]

When necessary, Sellar would point any accusers towards those who acquitted him on the day.

"Lord Pitmilly who presided over the minute investigation that lasted for 15 hours before a Jury of Highland gentlemen; Lord Cockburn, who then, as Counsel interrogated the witnesses and Culbockie, the foreman of the Jury are all alive, so is Home Drummond the King's Counsel.

> *They can tell how the case was sifted and how clear the villainous notice of the conspiracy was made out – that is, if necessary."* [STAFFORDSHIRE D593/P122]

Sellar was utterly convinced that the proof of the clearance actions in Sutherland was for the common good.

> *"Let any person… view the inside of one of the new fisherman's stone cots at Loth – the man and his wife and young children weaving their nets around the winter fire. Let him contrast it with the sloth and poverty and filth of an unremoved tenants turf in the interior."* [Loch]

And, he might have expected some support from the Sutherland Estate, given his record.

> *"If Lord and Lady Stafford have one tenant more industrious and improving or one more dutiful and loyal to them – one who in twice the time has extended of his own capital one half of my outlays on such a place, I shall be silent."* [STAFFORDSHIRE D593]

In fact in 1815 he effectively offered his resignation in a letter to Earl Gower.

> *"…I have now so completely snugged the business of my department that Mr Young ought really to find no difficulty in carrying through both and by these*

means a considerable saving in the management should happen. This is the fifth year of my collection…Lord and Lady Stafford and your Lordship will perhaps then permit me to resign my office, though not my humble claim on your good opinion." [Adam]

One of the major sources of criticism of both Sellar and the Sutherland Estate was the newspaper the Military Register. Produced in London and widely believed to have had its information supplied from within the heart of the old Sutherland establishment, the Military Register only saw one viewpoint and they attacked Sellar mercilessly. William Young summed up the mood as to the newspaper's approach.

"He (Sellar) had come to the estate to "do good not evil, yet the Apostle Paul would not convince the publisher of the Military Register or the people of this truth." [NLS DEP 313]

"The Military Register was one of the infernal spirits who rouse the poor and ignorant wretches to rebellion merely from sinister motives."[STAFFORDSHIRE D593/K]

James Loch, maybe hopefully, considered that the Military Register was not having too wide an influence.

"The Military Register was literally unknown anywhere but in Sutherland where it tended to keep the minds of the people unsettled and in a state of irritation."[Loch]

Books, newspaper and journal articles were being published that took a critical view of the clearances in Sutherland and Sellar's Strathnaver activities were held up as the example of their inhumanity.

Major General David Stewart of Garth in his extensive history of the Highland Clans ('Sketches of the Character, manners and Present State of the Highlands of Scotland') presented his assessment.

"The trial ended (as was expected by every person who understood the circumstance) in the acquittal of the acting agent, the verdict of the jury proceeding on the principle that he acted under legal authority. This acquittal, however, did by no means diminish the general feeling of culpability; it only transferred the offence from the agent to a quarter too high and too distant to be directly affected by public indignation, if indeed there be any station so elevated or so distant that public indignation justly excited will not sooner or later reach, so as to touch the feelings however obtuse of the transgressor of that law of humanity written on every upright mind." [Stewart]

Needless to say, Sellar was ready with his response writing decisively to Stewart, enclosing a copy of his own 'Statement'

Twenty years later Sellar was still answering his accusers.

> *To Editor of Tait's magazine 20th September 1847 – "observing by an extract of your treatise on the Highland clans which is inserted in the Weekly Register of the 8th current that you have stated as facts concerning me, several matters which are untrue, I take leave to wait upon you with the enclosed paper of which I beg your perusal. I published it one and twenty years ago in consequence of General Stewart of Garth having been misinformed, as you have been, and having misrepresented transactions which were under my charge and all the facts concerning which had been fully ascertained by a British jury and disposed of ten years preceding this date. I refer pointedly to persons, dates, documents and records and shew that it was not only most clearly proven at the time but admitted that those things on which you found in defamation of my character were as they now are 'absolute falsehoods' which were got up for a villainous and dishonest purpose… As you have unintentionally, I am sure, mis-stated so many facts concerning me, I trust that you will do me the justice to publish in your number for October, this letter and its enclosure and to make an apology for the errors into which you have fallen." [STAFFORDSHIRE D593/P/20]*

The ongoing clamour to hold Sellar up as a scapegoat for the Sutherland Clearances ensured he had to continue his vigilance, but he refused to let it prevent him from expanding his sheep empire. He bought new territory in Morvern, Argyllshire demonstrating his success and relative wealth. Still the press pack sought him out and used a report of the Queen's visit to Argyllshire to again highlight Sellar's past. In this instance The Times also made a direct link to the Sutherland family and estate, which gave Sellar the perfect opportunity to subtly remind 'His Grace' that he might expect their support.

> *"Your Grace has no doubt seen the unprovoked abuse, which The Times has poured out at me in their late number, which reported the Queen's progress through the County of Argyll. Entirely unprovoked it is, for I interfere with nothing beyond the private management of my own affairs, in which I support a great number of work people and I have brought into proper cultivation in this country better than 160 acres of tillage land which I am dressing, fencing and manuring so as to make it yield, if I can, a profitable venture. As the Times mentions the Sutherland family and may very possibly although I hope not, continue this abuse, I take the liberty to send your Grace a copy of the 'statement' which I published more than twenty years ago in case it may be wanted in any reference to facts.*
>
> *I wish also to mention to your Grace that in whatever state of independence it has pleased a kind providence to place a humble man like me, a great part of that independence has been derived from a rental of something like £1000 a*

year, which my father left me 30 years ago and the accumulation of which (since I lived entirely on my own industry) amounts to a considerable sum.

This accumulation and the legitimate profits flowing from farms industriously managed and paying to your Grace better than £2000 a year abundantly accounts for all my undertakings.

I will say it that in these undertakings as well under your Grace, as in this country and in Morayshire; and as well as in other people's affairs as in the rearing and educating my family, I have studied to act the part of an industrious honest man and a good subject.

When they tried themselves to the uttermost they could not show a single malpractice, scarce by an error into which I had fallen; and it would be very hard if in the present state of society such a tyrant as the Times is entitled, falsely to accuse an innocent person, an without prosecution to abuse that person with all the bitterness in its power.

I think of consulting Sir David Dundas whether there is no means to put an end to such tyranny. If these be, I feel that I have courage to adopt it; but I shall act with the soundest advice I can obtain.

All the land that I hold in this country I found in the possession sheep farmers who had it under Black Face sheep. My speculation is by substantial improvement and careful management to make it capable of producing cheviots and in the course of that speculation I divide more money among work people than all the proprietors in that district put together. In this year I have kept on a squad of men who otherwise must have been fed from public charity, and I furnished them with what meal they wanted, 6/- per Boll under the current prices. In this I know I fall short of your Grace and Mr Matheson's charities but I toppled over most men of my own humble calibre.

What they allude to of my favouring emigration is that at a meeting of our parochial board here, on its being shown to us that a great many persons resided in the parish who never had any thing betwixt them and starvation beyond the planting of a few barrels of potatoes. I pressed on the other gentlemen present how much these poor things were in a false position and the necessity of our doing something substantial to alleviate such distress. I offered as my [?] £50 if they would try to form a fund for the gradual transmission of these people either to where manufacturers would furnish work for them or where on the shores of the Canadian lakes lands of the very best quality to aid the occupancy of new settlers.

It is not hard that a man so industriously employed and so unobtrusive as I have always been should in a free country like this be subject to the loosest of all tyrannies that of an unprincipled and democratical press!

Knowing your Grace's goodness of heart I [?] these facts to you thinking it probable that you will in charity put me right in my present distress with her Grace the Duchess, Lord Ellesmere, the Duke of Norfolk, the Marquis of Westminster and Lord Morpeth to whom I had the honour to become known through your Grace's noble family, and also with the Duke and Duchess of Argyll to whom I also have the hounour to be known and who I understand are now on a visit to your Grace. I beg your Grace's pardon for intruding this long letter." [STAFFORDSHIRE D593/P120]

Sellar's ongoing notoriety was then, helping to bring unwanted attention on to the Sutherland Estate and therefore as a consequence one of Britain's most important noble families. The Countess of Sutherland was moved to comment.

"We have lately been much attacked by the newspapers by a few malicious writers who have long assailed us on every occasion.
What is stated is most perfectly unjust and unfounded as I am convinced of the facts I am acquainted with." [NLS DEP 313]

The affair was drawing the attention of some notable persons. Karl Marx in Das Kapital wrote,

"From 1814 to 1820, 15,000 inhabitants, about 3,000 families were systematically hunted and rooted out… Thus the fine Lady appropriated 794,000 acres of land that had from time immemorial belonged to the Clan. She assigned to the expelled unhabitants about 6,000 acres on the seashore."
[Mark 'Das Kapital']

Surprisingly a regular correspondent and flatterer of the Countess, Sir Walter Scott even weighed in with some criticism.

"In too many instances the Highlands have been drained not only of their superfluity of population, but of the whole mass of the inhabitants

dispossessed by an unrelenting avarice which will one day be found to have
been as short sighted as it is unjust and selfish."

One unlikely supporter of the Sutherland family and by association, Patrick Sellar was the anti-slavery advocate and author of 'Uncle Tom's Cabin', Harriet Beecher Stowe.

She was so impressed by the Sutherland family that she included in her 'Sunny Memories' a somewhat cloying critique of their actions.

"An almost sublime instance of the benevolence employed of superior wealth and
power in shortening the struggles of advancing civilisation and elevating in a few
years a whole community to a point of education and material prosperity which
unassisted they might never have attained." [Stowe]

This was just too much for the man who was probably to become Sellar's and the Sutherland Family's most persistent accuser. Donald MacLeod's lengthy series of letters, originally published in the newspapers, and then later in direct response to Harriet Beecher Stowe's publication as 'Gloomy Memories' is a detailed personal eye-witness account of the Strathnaver clearances. That he was present is not disputed, yet it was many years after the events before he chose to make his story known.

"I was an eye witness of the scene — strong parties led by Sellar and Young commenced setting fire to the dwellings till about 300 houses were in flames, the people striving to remove the sick, the helpless, before the fire should reach them. The cries of women and children — the roaring of cattle — the barking of dogs — the smoke of the fire — the soldiers — it required to be seen to be believed!"
[MacLeod, 'Gloomy Memories']

James Loch had long been employed by Lord Stafford to deal with all business and publicity affairs. Loch keenly embraced this role for the Sutherland properties on Lord Stafford's rise to fame as the 1st Duke of Sutherland. Loch shirked nothing and would vigorously defend the Estate at all and every opportunity.

"In giving the following account of the humane and considerate views which have regulated the management of this great and rapidly improving property no further notice will be taken of these mis-statements, except in as far as may be necessary to show what they are here stated distinctly to be totally and completely false. "Avoid a certain ironical expression which does you more mischief than you are aware of. The same is the case when you speak to the Highlanders both of the better and of the lower ranks." [STAFFORDSHIRE D593/K/1]

The Countess was also working her charms and intrigue in ensuring that those who could, gave out the right messages.

"Dined Dr Bethune, Ross of Clyne, Young and Sellar and Mackenzie of Farr. He gives an account of his parish with much tact, information and connaissance de cause…He was prudent in not saying anything of his own guesses and suspicions and stated only the facts he knew as if upon a sort of evidence but from his manner one could see what he thought… He is ready to contradict the false statements in the papers from his own knowledge." [Adam]

And if intrigue would not work, she would readily resort to outright threats. The Countess clearly expected ministers MacKenzie and Sage to pass on her expectations.

"For their own sakes the necessity of their remaining quiet in their own habitations and conforming with a due spirit of order and submission to the laws they ought to be warned of the consequences that will ensue to themselves from a contrary line of conduct and to be made acquainted that we are determined on the most decided perseverance in the plans laid down for the benefit of the country and the estate and that their own prosperity will depend upon their observance of order and good behaviour and above all things how necessary it is to observe in their future conduct strict adherence to truth, a true regard to the ninth commandment which I observe with concern is too little regarded among them as has of late appeared. I trust you will take every method for the sake of all concerned to explain our intentions to them and the absolute necessity that they should direct their attention to a proper conduct on their parts

that they may have no excuse in the future of being unwarned on the subject."
[STAFFORDSHIRE D593/K1/5/5]

Even although the people finally were to be rid of Sellar as their factor his effect lingered long and Donald MacLeod's emotive prose kept the events in prominence.

"The removal of Messrs Young and Sellar, particularly the latter, from the power they had exercised so despotically, was hailed with the greatest joy by the people, to whom their vary names were a terror. Their appearance in any neighbourhood had been such a cause of alarm, as to make women fall into fits, and in one instance caused a woman to lose her reason whenever she saw a stranger she cried out with a terrific tone and manner – Oh there's Sellar."
[MacLeod 'Gloomy Memories']

Chapter 6

GUILTY BY ASSOCIATION

When they tried themselves to the uttermost they could not show a single malpractice.
Patrick Sellar

If one thing is clear amongst the maze of accusations and counter accusations it is that no one single hand acted in isolation and without the knowledge and maybe collusion of others. The personal vendettas, the politics of the day, and the intransigence of many, all helped to muddy the waters. Time it seems does not make it all that clearer.

Patrick Sellar however was the only one of the players to be legally called to account. The Justiciary accepted that there was a legal case to answer.

Lord Pitmilly, after having stated the law as applicable to this case, summed up the evidence in a very clear and able manner. His lordship stated, that it was unnecessary for the jury to consider any of the charges, excepting the one in regard to the old woman at Badinloskin. As to the first, there could be no doubt of the practice in the country, of retaining these barns till the crops would be threshed out; neither could it be doubted, that Mr. Sellar had not left the whole

91

of the barns for the use of the outgoing tenants, and in consequence of this, the tenants suffered damage. But in Point of law, as the Court of Session had decided in a similar question, Mr. Sellar was not bound by any such practice, but was entitled to proceed in the ejections. In regard to the injury charged to have been done to Margaret McKay, his Lordship directed the attention of the jury to the evidence of Chisholm. This witness, although contradicted in some particulars by his wife, was confirmed by John McKay, whose testimony his Lordship also laid before them. On the other hand, he brought under their view, the evidence of Sutherland, Fraser, and Burns, and stated that it was the duty of the Jury to balance betwixt these two sets of witnesses. His Lordship also said, that if the jury were at all at a loss on this part of the case, they ought to take into view he character of the accused; for this was always of importance in balancing contradictory testimony. Now here there was, in the first place, real evidence, from the conduct of Mr. Sellar, in regard to the sick, for this, in several instances, had been proved to be most humane.

And secondly, there were the letters of Sir George Abercromby, Mr. Brodie, and Mr. Fenton, which, although not evidence, must have some weight with the jury; and there were the testimonies of Mr. Gilzean and Sir Archibald Dunbar—all establishing Mr. Sellar's humanity of disposition. [Robertson]

Sellar's actions and thinking are only really available through the archives of others and these are generally very 'public' pronouncements in his own hand. His private papers are at best missing but in all probability up in smoke.

Family convention and local legends suggest that there was a family trend to light bonfires upon the death of their loved ones. Local legend records such a conflagration at Ardtornish, Sellar's property in Argyll, and his grandson the writer and historian Andrew Lang, left instructions in his will for his papers to be burned – a strange act for a committed historian unless there was something to hide! It is interesting that Prof. Richards seems to have uncovered some family materials in Australia, where the Lang's continue to live.

Patrick Sellar claimed his innocence to the last.

> *"Not one hut or one stick of single hut on the ground taken possession by me was burned by any person in my employ." [Adam]*

Horace Fairhurst's 20th Century archaeological excavations, obviously not available at the time of the trial, seem to back up Sellar's assertion.

> *Our own problem arises from the fact that we found no evidence that the buildings we excavated had been burnt; admittedly only a small sample was examined but a careful study was made with this point in mind as the name of Rosal specifically has been quoted as an example of Sellar's ferocity. [Fairhurst]*

The inhabitants of Strathnaver were in fact 'legally' removed after due process had been executed and apparently the agreement of the people themselves.

> *"After repeated promises by the tenants that they would peaceably obey the Sheriff's decreet and after they repeatedly failed in implementing their promises I was under the necessity of directing the officers to execute their warrants."* [Richards 'Patrick Sellar and the Highland Clearances']

Sellar remained adamant that he was the salvation of the common people.

> *"There is no part of my conduct as your factor which can cause a friend I have to blush, to see the account printed and posted on the market cross. They never were kept to their text in any one point until I came among them. They have no hope while I am your servant for they know they cannot cheat me."* [Richards 'Patrick Sellar and the Highland Clearances']

He had the backing of the Countess, at least in the beginning.

> *"The tenants expect that the estate should be given away to them and at the same time without any prospect of profit to themselves. It would be a positive gain to get rid of this inefficient people."* [Richards, 'Patrick Sellar and the Highland Clearances']

Sellar may have attempted to mitigate some of the accusations. James Loch showed little sympathy.

> *"You say you are aware you have made many enemies by doing your duty. Believe me the number of enemies a man makes by doing his duty steadily and honestly are very few, the mode of doing it however, makes the case very different." [Adam]*

At best Sellar had apparently learned nothing and at worst showed no remorse. At the earliest opportunity he sought to engage in the next batch of removals. James Loch, now chief commissioner of the Sutherland Estate stepped in.

> *"Your ideas are impossible unless the Marquis and Lady Stafford depart from their present wise system of not to turn out a single inhabitant against whom crimes have not been proven until a situation on the coast is pointed out." [Adam]*

Donald Sage's account of the 1819 Clearances however show that Sellar proceeded to act as before.

> *"The clearances of 1819 seemed to have only been approved by the outcome of the trial – The middle of the week brought on the day of the Strathnaver clearance. At an early hour of that day Mr Sellar, accompanied by the Fiscal, and escorted by a strong body of constables, sheriff officers and others,*

commenced work at Grummore. Their plan of operations was to clear the
cottages of their inmates, giving them about half an hour to pack up and carry
off their furniture, and then set the cottages on fire.

To this plan they ruthlessly adhered without the slightest regard to any obstacle
that might arise. At Grumbeg lived a soldier's widow, Henny Munro. When
Sellar came to the widow's house, Henny stood up to plead for her furniture.
She was told with an oath that if she did not take her trumpery off within half
an hour it would be burned. The poor widow had only to task the remains of
her bodily strength and address herself to the work of dragging her sheets, beds,
presses and stools out of the door and placing them at the gable of her cottage.
No sooner was her task accomplished than the torch was applied. The wind
blew in the direction of the furniture and the flame lighting upon it, speedily
reduced it to ashes. A worse fate awaited the mother-in-law of Samuel
Matheson. She lived at Rhimisdale, and had been reduced to such a state of
bodily weakness that she could neither walk nor lie in bed. She could only night
and day sit in her chair. Many people represented to Sellar the special difficulty
of removing Bean Roaomasdail.

They were told that she must immediately be removed by her friends or the
constables would be ordered to do it. The good wife of Rhimisdale was therefore
raised by her weeping family from her chair and laid on a blanket the corners of
which were held up by four of the strongest youths in the place. All this she bore
with meekness. The change of posture and the rapid movement of the bearers
however awakened a most intense pain and her cries never ceased till with a few
miles of her destination when she fell asleep. A week later I travelled through the

area. The banks of the lake and the river, formerly studded with cottages, now met the eye as a scene of desolation. Of all the houses the thatched roofs were gone; but the walls, built of alternate layers of turf and stone remained. The flames of the preceding week still slumbered in the ruins. The sooty rafters of the cottages as they were being consumed filled the air with a heavy and most offensive odour." [Sage]

By 1817 the Countess was also expressing concerns to Loch over Sellar's post acquittal plans.

"We must not give him [Sellar] any promise of entry unless sure of being able to keep it. Sellar is too sly and refining upon his plans by concealing half." [Grimble]

Others in or around the scene knew the true extent of Patrick Sellar's clearing activities.

Going public was however not an option for many. Their own position with the Sutherland Estate could be in jeopardy if they were seen to take sides. Given the accepted and known venom with which Sellar could apply the law for his own ends may also have kept some quiet.

Comments in letters, however, give a clearer picture of what was suspected if not known as to Sellar's behaviour and possible guilt. James Loch was hedging his bets a bit when writing to his uncle and Chief Commissioner of the Jury Court in Scotland.

> *"The witnesses are a set of people whose education and rank of life entitle them to little credit unless supported by other evidence. While I state this I am far from thinking that Sellar has not acted hastily and unadvisedly but that he has been guilty of the crimes (even that of murder) that are insinuated rather than alleged by MacKid against him I totally disbelieve and I look upon them as pure offspring of jealousy and ill nature."* [Richards 'Patrick Sellar and the Highland Clearances']

Loch expanded,

> *"Sellar is a clever Scotch writer a man full of energy which activity has necessarily been often called for to enforce very disagreeable but very necessary acts of vigour added to which he has a quick sneering biting way of saying good things in the execution of his duty which I do not think has made him popular with anybody whether in the management of the affairs or otherwise."* [Richards 'Patrick Sellar and the Highland Clearances']

Loch finally gave vent to his feelings about Patrick Sellar. Sellar's persistent intention to carry on where he had left off saw Loch write to the Lady Stafford.

> *"Sellar is a man possessing less discrimination than it is easy to believe and was really guilty of many very oppressive and cruel acts.*
>
> *In whatever related to the intercourse or management of the men or to the knowledge or conduct of the world or above all to a gentlemanly feeling of understanding, he is deficient beyond measure. He is the most unfit person from these defects to be entrusted with the management and therefore with the character of any ancient and distinguished family." [STAFFORDSHIRE D593/K]*

Patrick Sellar's one time sponsor, George MacPherson Grant, now came forward to present a view of the man, quite different from his initial references.

> *"Sellar's advice carried too much very extraneous matter and his remarks upon many things shew that satirical turn which does him so much harm." [Adam]*

MacPherson Grant went on to turn the screw and effectively blamed Sellar for duping them all.

"He is quite a person when in daily communication with and very apt to make you forget the great and irredeemable defects of his character." [Richards 'Patrick Sellar and the Highland Clearances']

The Countess, herself claimed to have always recognised positive and negative factors in Sellar.

"Sellar was unpopular with the gentlemen (tacksmen) of the estate, but he understands managing the common people… the people and things seem to flourish and to be happy and contented." [NLS DEP 313]

The Rev. David Mackenzie, a man with a number of masters vying to influence his conscience was tempted in a letter to James Loch to suggest that there was no smoke without fire.

"The circumstances regarding Mr Sellar … have a foundation, however highly exaggerated." [Richards 'Leviathan of Wealth']

One man who certainly knew more truths than most was Robert MacKid. Yet his long-standing animosity towards Sellar and his ultimate downfall and grovelling apology makes him a witness of dubious veracity. MacKid was Sheriff Substitute for the County of Sutherland and the person given responsibility for investigating the charges – charges in Sellar's opinion that were not only obviously made up, they were the work of his enemies.

> *"The precognition was bound to be a tissue of misrepresentations against me because of McKid's ill will towards me and because of his manipulation of the Gaelic speaking witnesses…The specific complaint made to Lady Stafford at the end of July 1814 was six weeks after the original episode.*
> *It was virtually incredible that much graver offences (such as murder) would have been withheld at that time. Would my accusers have suppressed these more heinous circumstances now brought against me if such circumstance had really existed." [Richards, 'Patrick Sellar and the Highland Clearances']*

Sellar's contention was that MacKid, in particular, but along with others was instrumental in using the vulnerable peasants to settle their scores.

> *"Mr McKid must know me to be innocent but he hopes to ruin my character and to injure my fortune by subjecting me to odium, trouble and expense. The ignorant people had been stimulated by artful and designing men to complain of oppression." [Adam]*

However, whether Robert MacKid was the prime mover or not, it should be recognised this action was supported by the people of Strathnaver and in that, it was a unique form of resistance.

Where resistance did happen in response to evictions it normally took the form of physical resistance – recourse to the law was a new approach.

Nevertheless, Robert MacKid was to become the scapegoat. The legal establishment lined up to effectively blame MacKid. William MacKenzie, the Countesses Edinburgh lawyer said.

> *"Sellar's conduct has been rash and more keen than necessary but McKid had brought himself into a serious scrape which will probably end in his ff. McKid has been extremely irregular if not absolutely illegal." [NLS DEP 313]*

MacKid had sought advice from his superior, Sheriff Cranstoun. Cranstoun's reply on 13th May 1815 was maybe not what MacKid wanted to hear and he certainly doesn't seem to have paid much heed to its recommendations.

> *"I am confident that you will extricate yourself with your usual ability and good sense. I do not think that you should begin with committing Sellar. The statements of Highlanders are often so false and exaggerated that a judicial engaging ought to be made before a step of that kind is taken. Proceed first with the precognition, then take Sellar's declaration and if there is ground for a criminal proceeding commit afterwards.*

I am very clearly of the opinion that the charge does not amount to wilful fire raising in the sense in which that would be used in the law of Scotland, as a capital crime. If Sellar is therefore committed the offence is certainly bailable and the usual bail for a person in his circumstances must be taken. Have no extra-judicial communication with Sellar. Do not let him be present at the precognition of the other witnesses... and if further engaging is necessary in consequence of his explanations, re-examine the witnesses." [National Archives of Scotland CS232 1. D. S23/2]

The trial Judge, Lord Pitmilly, among his many less than impartial comments also laid the blame on MacKid.

"I am perfectly satisfied with Sellar's acquittal, having realised how evident it was there existed a combination against him and that MacKid had been at the bottom of it." [Richards 'Patrick Sellar and the Highland Clearances']

MacKid however claimed he was only doing his duty.

"I was induced to go into Strathnaver where at considerable inconvenience and expense and with much patient perseverance, I examined about 40 witnesses... and it is with deepest regret I have to inform your Lordship that a more numerous catalogue of crimes perpetrated by one individual has seldom disgraced any country or sullied the pages of a precognition in Scotland." [National Archives of Scotland SRO CS 232/S/23/2]

Patrick Sellar and Robert MacKid had 'history' that went back to their days in Moray. MacKid it appears worked for Thomas Sellar's legal business in Elgin. Thomas, Patrick's father, is recognised as a respected man and having a business conducive to training newly qualified 'writers'. Somewhere in this period the two clashed and the animosity between the two festered and flared on various occasions.

In 1811 Sellar found an opportunity to highlight what he claimed was McKid's poor management of the Road Fund.

> "Four fifths of the fund have not been collected and the situation was in the worst state possible. Mr. McKid, the JP, is blamed and I know he is indolent but this was to so many an unpleasant subject that I suppose he had not been pushed to his duty." [To Earl Gower) – "the poor man is not in good health and in low spirits. He has given up a business in Ross-shire for a £90 salary in Sutherland, which together with a small farm permitted him an idle life. And instead of building a stance of good offices he has built himself a castle. He lived there a life of much indolence and inattention." [NLS DEP 313]

Sellar continued to blacken MacKid at every opportunity. MacKid had been accused of poaching and Sellar took delight in informing his employers of his 'catch'.

"This morning just as the people were collecting with their rents Mr Nash brought me an information against Mr MacKid for poaching and I took the liberty to write to your Ladyship a hurried note with it. I have had no return from MacKid to me note and I fain hope that the information may have been in some degree incorrect; for nothing could be more mean than for a gentleman to kill a proprietor's game in the snow and without being qualified by licence or leave of the landlord. However the informant who is one of our police has been here tonight offering his affidavit and claiming his guinea; and I suspect Mr MacKid has been very foolish as to run his head into this scrape." [Adam]

And he took every opportunity to remind the Marchioness of MacKid's fall from grace.

"Your ladyship will recollect that I took him over the coals in Spring 1811 and that we passed it over as a thing incredible of a gentleman in his office."
[Patrick Sellar]

Sellar's ultimate aim was to rid Sutherland of MacKid – something he was eventually to achieve following his acquittal. Sellar knew the danger to himself from MacKid and urged the Estate to replace him.

"McKid is a clever man without sense or principle if the country were clear of him and a moderate modest man in his shoes it would be well"
"He is determined to take revenge on us by breaches of trust in which he could

105

keep within the letter of the law and so do us much annoyance." [NLS DEP 313]

Eventually Sellar was persuaded on the advice of among others, his father, to take the least painful course of action against MacKid. In a letter to George MacPherson Grant, Sellar writes:

> *"Dear Sir, From the nature of the advice you were so good to give me, last year, respecting MacKid and the interest you have always been so kind as take in what concerned me, I venture to intrude on you with the annexed copy of the correspondence by which I have settled my suit against him – I found the miserable man involved in such difficulties on all hands and his family of I believe 9 or 10 young children so constantly about to be beggared by my bringing him to trial that I was pleased to wash my hands of him." [STAFFORDSHIRE D593/K/1/3/5]*

MacKid, was by this stage largely helpless and to satisfy Sellar's honour and spare himself and his family further suffering he was induced to write a letter of retraction.

> *"Being impressed with the perfect conviction and belief that the statements to your prejudice, contained in the precognition which I took in Strathnaver in May 1815 were to such an extent exaggerations as to amount to falsehoods, I am free to admit that, led away by the clamour excited against you, on account of the discharge of the duties of our office, as factor for the Marchioness of Sutherland,*

in introducing a new system of management on the Sutherland estate, I gave a degree of credit to those mis-statements of which I am now thoroughly ashamed, and which I most sincerely and deeply regret.

From the aspersions thrown on your character I trust you need not doubt that you are already fully acquitted in the eyes of the world. That you would be entitled to exemplary damages from me for my participation in the injury done you I am most sensible and I shall therefore not only acknowledge it as most important obligation conferred on me and my innocent family, if you will have the goodness to drop your law suits against me, but I shall also pay the expenses of that suit and place at your disposal towards the reimbursement of the provisional expenses which this most unfortunate business has occasioned to you any sum you may exact when made acquainted with of my affairs trusting to your generosity to have consideration to the heavy expenses my defence has cost me and that my connection with the unfortunate affair has induced me to resign the office Sheriff Substitute of Sutherland." [STAFFORDSHIRE D593/K/1/3/5]

Sellar was now in a position to appear magnanimous as he replied to Robert MacKid's agent, Joseph Gordon.

"Dear Sir I have instantly received through your hands Mr MacKid's letter to me of this date and have heard from you an explanation of the state of his affairs (which as he is no longer possessed of the power illegally to deprive a British subject of his liberty and therewith to oppress him under the form of law) induce

me from compassion to Mr MacKid's family to drop my suit against him on his paying the whole expenses of the said suit and placing at my disposal two hundred pounds sterling and having just received your obligation as security for Mr MacKid's performance of this I cheerfully give this authority for dismissing the process From this moderation with which I have acted towards your client in this affair you will believe I am sure that I have no wish to distress Mrs MacKid and her family and her commissions by any publication on the subject in the newspapers at same time.

I have explained to you that such publication may happen in the course of the trial of the particulars in this affair without my being able to prevent it."
[STAFFORDSHIRE D593/K/1/3/5]

The Countess endorsed the rights of his downfall.

"MacKid's character has now been "quite blown" he "had been exciting the people against us" preying on "the democratic feeling all these people have in spite of themselves" [NLS DEP 313]

Interestingly, a neighbouring landowner, George Dempster of Skibo, who was respected for some of his forward thinking and innovative methods in dealing with his tenants[2], also weighed in

---

[2] At Skibo, through the 'Constitution of Creich', Dempster set about ensuring farm tenants and their families long-term security with positive incentives for the management and improvement of their grounds, thereby improving their living standards. Dempster's abolition of feudalism was far advanced for his time.

against MacKid. Writing to Lady Stafford he made his feeling quite plain.

> *"Congratulations on the news that we are likely to get rid of a very great and long complained of nuisance in Sutherlandshire, in the person of Mr MacKid as Sheriff Substitute…. Perfectly convinced as I am that he has been the secret but chief promoter and publisher of all the unpleasant disturbances in the county that have lately attracted so much notice in the public. MacKid has shown me inveterate hostility ever since I refused a tenancy on the Skibo estate."* [NLS DEP 313]

Never one to pass up an opportunity, on the dismissal of MacKid, Sellar suggested that he would make a perfect replacement as Sheriff Substitute for Sutherland. George MacPherson Grant, confidant and advisor to the Staffords was quick to point out that this would not be a good decision!

> *"It would be a foundation for insinuating that MacKid was sacrificed to Sellar's accommodation and the present impression of MacKid's undermining him would revert upon himself."* [NLS DEP 313]

Sellar tried one final throw in his humiliation of Robert MacKid by offering to lease MacKid's now departed farm at Kirkton. James Loch wanted no further opportunity for public criticism.

"In every point of view this would have been quite ruinous to the estate and the future management - Sellar has enough land already. It shews much too greedy a disposition on Sellar's part." [STAFFORDSHIRE D593/K]

Robert MacKid became a victim of the whole Strathnaver episode. To some extent it seems he was a victim of his own actions.

It seems highly likely that he let his feud with Patrick Sellar determine and hasten his actions. Mackid was given the task of collecting the statements from the Strathnaver tenants only because his 'boss', Sheriff Cranstoun was unavailable at the time. Nevertheless he must have seen the Strathnaver tenants complaint as an opportunity to gather some 'mud' about Sellar. The harrowing stories he heard from the Strathnaver people may have galvanised him into the passion that saw him arrest and against advice imprison Patrick Sellar in Dornoch Jail.

What remains unknown is if and to what extent Robert MacKid fuelled the complaints that ultimately led to the trial. His name was certainly associated with the 'intelligence' being reported by the Military Register. Robert MacKid was bankrupted by his involvement in the affair and forced to ignominiously remove himself and his family to Thurso.

The Duchess/Countess might have claimed some immunity from guilt in terms of having a 'distant' view, but all the evidence points towards a woman who having been brought up with intrigue and suspicion, made sure she knew exactly what was being done. Delegation to 'trusted' managers would have been essential in terms of simply getting things done, but this shrewd woman missed nothing. Sellar himself confirmed this when writing to the Countess.

> *"My Lady*
>
> *As not a mouse stirs in Sutherland without Your Grace hearing of it…"*
> *[STAFFORDSHIRE 593/K/1/3/26]*

The 'establishment' and the landowning gentry, maybe naturally, supported the view that the Duke and Duchess only ever intended good for their tenants. Lady Stafford's regular advisor, George MacPherson Grant was one to come to the family's defence.

> *"The 'family' wanted above all else the improvement and happiness of the people, and that in inducing them to adopt more industrious habits as well, as little as possible should be done to hurt their feelings, both for their sakes and the success of the measures themselves." [Richards 'Patrick Sellar and the Highland Clearances']*

Sellar of course was happy to agree and noted that without the good grace and kindness of the Sutherland Estate, the people would have been doomed.

> *"They cannot raise provisions for their own consumption insomuch that they must have perished but for your Ladyship's bounty. Their unavailing efforts for that which they are not fitted has damped and depressed their industry. Your Ladyship had lulled asleep their care… they have sunk into despondent security."* [Patrick Sellar]

The Sutherland Family was certainly culpable in their failure to meet parts of their end of the bargain. The people of Strathnaver were to be provided with new plots of land on the coastal fringes. William Young, the head factor, explained the delay was caused by:

> *"The illness of the surveyor's wife, but by the 4th June everything was ready for the reception of the people."* [NLS DEP 313]

Young went on to admit this as a failure, but in a letter to James Loch while acknowledging that the people were disadvantaged, true to character he exonerated himself.

> *"The Strathnaver people certainly got too short notice and should have had longer time to move off, I admit it, but the fault was none of mine and had Roy*

the land surveyor's advice been listened to the thing would not have happened."
[Adam]

James Loch also came close to an admission of some Sutherland Estate responsibility.

> *"Much discontent exists (and it is well founded) in these districts and especially in Strathnaver in consequence of the people who have been removed from the valley from their various habitations in the hills, having been thrown into one common lot, without any division having been made. This state of things must have tended to keep alive that feeling of regret and disquietude which that sudden and not well digested removal from the hills in the first instance induced."*
> *[Loch]*

The ground in question may have been surveyed by this time but there was little or no provision made for the incoming population. William Young laid the ultimate blame at Sellar's door.

> *"The sheep farmers expected too large a financial return and that too quickly, even in the first summer of their leases. Our friend Sellar ought to have known this, but dearly he has paid for his rashness."* *[NLS DEP 313]*

One of the greatest disappointments felt by the people of Sutherland was the Countesses failure to honour the commitment to provide land and a living for returning soldiers – soldiers that had signed up based on the traditional bond between the people and the Countess as head of their clan. The failure to honour this tradition was seen as particularly hurtful.

Even where some measure of compassion had been provided this was rapidly withdrawn from the family upon the death of the soldier. A Widow Bannerman of Gartymore was quoted in the Inverness Courier.

> *"My husband, Quartermaster Sergeant, a native of Sutherland, returned home when discharged from the 93rd Regiment after serving 23 years. He came to Gartymore and paid the outgoing tenant £60 value of the house. On his decease, I was ejected with my two fatherless children, helpless bedridden girls and refused the valuation money of the house. The Duke's officer came with a strong party and threw out our furniture and then cut the couples and let the roof into the house before we could get shelter of a house." [Inverness Courier]*

The tradition of military service at the call of the head of the clan was something the people believed in and up to this point anyway, the people of Sutherland had always responded when the call to arms came With their faith in the Countess now somewhat diminished, Patrick Sellar's contribution to the debate, when he wrote to Lord Stafford, could not have helped.

"They are a race of people, living in barbarous sloth and filth, breeding men for the recruiting sergeant." [NLS DEP 313]

One, George Mackay, drew up a petition that echoed this disappointment with their Countess.

"I and my predecessors have lived comfortably and happily under the worthy and ever to be esteemed family of Sutherland from time immemorial. I and my forebears brought up families on their small farms with satisfaction and comfort to themselves, useful members of society, a heroic and able race well calculated for the service of their King and Country. That to annihilate such a race (while they are at the will, desire and disposal of their esteemed proprietor), the petitioner is confident never was the intention of the family of lady Stafford" I now find myself thus driven from the place of my nativity in the utmost distress without knowing where to go with my small family." [Richards 'Patrick Sellar & the Highland Clearances]

Among the accusations against Sellar had been the setting fire to the heath and thereby destroying any crops and grazing that was essential to maintaining the crofters meagre lifestyles. Now Sellar was claiming that he was only following custom and as such it was his and the Estates prerogative to do so. Hugh Miller was later to put a slightly different light on the applicability of the custom.

"In the month of March 1814 a large proportion of the Highlanders of Farr and Kildonan … were summoned to quit their farms the following May. In a few days after, the surrounding heaths on which they pastured their cattle, and from which at that season the sole supply of herbage is derived… were set on fire and burnt up. There was that sort of policy in the stroke that men deem allowable in a state of war. The starving cattle went roaming over the burnt pastures and found nothing to eat… Term day was suffered to pass. The work of demolition then began."[Miller]

But by what right did the Sutherland Estate have in pursuing such acts and processes? Hugh Miller, a vocal critic, laid the guilt squarely at the 'top table'.

"The Clearances exemplified a defect in the British Constitution…that the rights of property may be so stretched as to overbear the rights of conscience." *[Rosie]*

The church ministers have often been criticised for their tendency to 'toady' to the landowners as their benefactors. Their support, however tacit, was crucial if the Sutherland Estate was to succeed with their plans. The ministers were the Estate's main channels of communication – they spoke the Gaelic language of the people and as such were required to translate the English edicts and instructions being handed down by the landowners.

The people of Sutherland, like many others in the Highlands of the time, were deeply religious and looked to their ministers for guidance not just in spiritual ways but also in guiding them in their daily lives.

> *The babies died, and the young men sighed,*
> *And maids wrung the lily hand*
> *And time-stricken beldames grew stark mad*
> *As they watched the burning brand*
> *Yes! All that was dear to those Highland hearts*
> *To the flames gave fuel and food:*
> *Lady! weep not, the Church has said.*
> *The Duke did as he should*

The ministers were often in a position of 'damned if I do and damned if I don't'. They relied on the landowners for their living yet had to live with their consciences. Sellar certainly seemed to have found the ministers less than suitable for their assigned roles.

> *"The ministers are men bred in a country of sloth and idleness, the sons of Highland tenants and whisky smugglers and with a tone imbibed from earliest infancy of detestation of every introduction to industry and innovation in the ancient language and manner of the Gael. The Staffords should replace the*

ministers and schoolmasters with men from Aberdeen and Kincardineshire where
the people are extremely industrious." [Patrick Sellar]

The Military Register was also critical of the ministers, but whereas Sellar saw them as being too close in ways to the people, this dissident newspaper suggested the ministers were less than supportive of the people's plight.

"The Ministers of the meek, Jesus, of whatever country or persuasion are never
less appropriately employed than when lending themselves in any shape directly
or indirectly to acts of inhumanity – and the people of Farr do say 'David, thou
art the man'." [Military Register 11th October 1815]

The Rev David MacKenzie played a central and often an arbitration role in the Strathnaver events. He carried out the instructions of the Countess in translating the various decisions that would affect the physical and social wellbeing of his parishioners; yet he sought to balance this with his genuine concern for their spiritual wellbeing.

The Rev. David MacKenzie had taken over the small mission at Achness, situated in the midst of Sellar's new sheep farm, in 1813. For two years before being translated to the Parish Church of Farr he was at the heart of the Strathnaver Clearances.

Then as minister to the wider Parish of Farr he found himself being pushed and pulled from all sides. The Countess expected him to 'toe the party line', the legal fraternity tried to engage him as an arbiter and his parishoners looked to him if not for salvation, certainly for spiritual and practical guidance.

Maybe more than most the Rev MacKenzie understood the life of the 'ordinary man' In his early years he had been employed in the mills at Spinningdale and only graduated from Kings College in 1810. During his holidays he worked as the parish schoolmaster at Tongue, so this was a man who lived among the native inhabitants of the area and understood the way of life.

> *"The people are social among themselves; kind and hospitable to strangers, according to their circumstances; acute and intelligent, according to their advantages; moral in their general habits; regular in attending on religious ordinances; and many among them decidedly pious."*

The Rev Mackenzie was accused by Donald Macleod in his 'Gloomy Memories' of being a 'puppet' of the Sutherland family but this accusation may have been fuelled by personal reasons. Rev. Mackenzie had at some point refused to sign a reference and certificate of good conduct for MacLeod.

Mackenzie himself insisted he did not fraternise and do the bidding of the Sutherland factors. He was however present at a dinner, attended by Sellar, at the house of Robert Gordon of Langdale on the eve of the first clearances. Gordon was however Mackenzie's father-in-law so he may well have been in the regular habit of dining at Langdale.

Mackenzie was defended to some extent during the Napier Commission's investigations when the Rev William Hall Telford presented a series of letters between MacKenzie and James Loch. Loch on promising Mackenzie a new Manse at Farr, suggested that Rev. MacKenzie should assure his congregation that their removals was done under "favourable terms" The minister's reply informed Loch that he had given.

> *"…publicity to his letter" but as to the process of "removing them from the upper parts of the Strath to the sea coast, then to leave them to depend for subsistence on the natural productiveness of their new stances, will not ameliorate their circumstances… there is no traffic, no industry, nor any opportunities for earning money by day labour." [STAFFORDSHIRE D593/K/1/3/6]*

On this basis the Rev. Mackenzie asked to be,

"…excused from giving any assurances of the change being to their advantage."[Mackay]

In his contribution to the New Statistical Account he provides a detailed appraisal of the changes.

"When the former account was written a considerable number of tacksmen, natives of this parish, occupied extensive farms in different parts of it; and with them, a dense population of subtenants resided in the interior straths and glens. Now however, all the lands, both hill and dale, which they possessed, are held in lease by a few sheep farmers, all non-resident gentlemen – some of them living in Caithness, some on the south coast of this county, and some in England; and the straths, in which hundreds of families lived comfortably are now tenanted by about twenty four families of herds. In place of the scores of Highland cattle, horses, sheep and goats, which formerly were brought to market or used for domestic purposes, now thousands of fleeces of Cheviot wool, wedders and ewes are annually exported. The people who had been removed from the interior in 1818 and 1819 when these great changes took place are thickly settled along the sea coast of the parish – in some instances about thirty lotters occupying the land formerly in the possession of twelve and some of them placed on ground which had been formerly uncultivated… The changes referred to in the locality and in the employment of the inhabitants have had their influence on the state of society in the parish. Although there are greater facilities of communication…the manners of the resident population are not thereby improved. It is a well

121

authenticated fact in this country, that the herring fishing is not conducive to the improvement of the morals of those engaged in it. The lease holders of our large sheep farms are as was already mentioned all non-resident gentlemen. But the former tacksmen resided on their own farms most of them having respectable and numerous families.

By their education and status in society…their example in their general intercourse with the people had an influence in giving a respectable tone to society, which is now almost gone." [New Statistical Account of Scotland Vol. XV]

As a possible arbiter the Rev Mackenzie was recognised as a natural 'man in the middle' and attempts were made to settle the Sellar dispute out of court through the minister. Sellar's prejudices against Mackenzie made this a non-starter.

"The Lord Advocate recruited me as an arbiter between Sellar and the Strathnaver people but I was regarded too much by Sellar as one of his many enemies and accused me of leaking the plan to the Military Register."

In 1843 he followed his conscience left the established Church of Scotland and joined the new Free Church as its minister at Farr.

Despite their sometimes support, the ministers were seen by some as compliant with the whole tragedy. Donald MacLeod (and others) were to highlight that the ministers abused their positions a spiritual leaders to subdue any rumblings of discontent and revolt by claiming that this was simply God repaying them for whatever sins they may have been committing.

> *"The splendid and comfortable mansions of these gentlemen were reddened with the glare of their neighbours flaming houses, without exciting any compassion for the sufferers…The clergy in their sermons maintained that the whole was a merciful interposition of providence to bring them to repentance, rather than send them all to hell as they richly deserved. And here I beg leave to ask…my late minister David Mackenzie of Farr, if it be true, as was generally reported that during these horrors there was a letter sent from the proprietors, addressed to him or to the general body requesting to know if the removed tenants were well provided for and comfortable or words to that effect and that the answer returned was that the people were quite comfortable in their new allotments and that the change was greatly to their benefit." [Macleod – Destitution in Sutherlandshire, 1819]*

Donald Sage one in an auspicious family line to act as minister to the people of Sutherland had his papers and records gathered together in the 1890 publication Memorabilia Domestica. The work is an account of social and religious life seen through the Sage eyes. While it is not the central theme of the book, a clear and unambiguous statement of responsibility is laid at the factors doors.

"This sweeping desolation extended over many parishes but it fell most heavily on the parish of Kildonan. It was the device of one William Young a successful corn dealer and land improver. Young has as his associate in the factorship a man of the name of Sellar, who acted in the subordinate capacity of legal agent and accountant on the estate, and who, by his unprincipled recklessness in conducting the process of ejectment, added fuel to the flame. A vast extent of moorland within the parishes of Farr and Kildonan was let to Mr Sellar, factor for the Stafford family, by his superior, as a sheep or store farm; the measure he employed to eject the poor, but original possessors of the lands was fire. At Rhimisdale, a township crowded with small tenants, a corn mill was set on fire in order effectually to scare the people from the place before the term of eviction arrived. Firing or injuring a corn mill, on which the sustenance of the lieges so much depends is or was by our ancient Scottish statutes punishable by imprisonment or civil banishment, and on this point of law Mr Sellar was ultimately tried." [Sage]

The Press of the day and in particular the Military Register were certainly guilty of stirring up public opinion and in the mind of some 'local' people were keeping 'the pot boiling' Among those claimed to be associated with and supplying the Military Register with information were members of the 'old order' This old hierarchy of Highland culture was being dismantled as part of the process of 'improvement' and many were naturally resistant to the loss of their status. Fuel for their fires of resentment might well have been providing newspaper copy.

> *"Sutherland of Scibbercross had been 'tampering with and exciting the people'.*

The Military Register, the investigative journal of the day and while hardly impartial proved itself on a number of occasions to have ready access to pertinent information.

> *"It was publicly stated in Sutherland that all the exculpatory witnesses were brought from Strathnaver were surreptitiously entertained at Sellar's house at Culmaily on their way to the trial. One of Sellar's witnesses had been decked out in a new suit of clothes." [Richards 'Military Register and the Pursuit of Patrick Sellar']*

Among the people themselves there were those who were employed by the Sutherland Estate and were 'obliged' to carry the burning torch. The Countess effectively pointed a finger of guilt at one of Sellar's torchbearers.

> *"From what I have seen and heard I am convinced he is innocent and has been correct and straightforward in what he has done and that the people are set on and not so much in it themselves. Sellar's only fault had been to employ*

Mathew Short as a shepherd. Short was a man with an unsavoury record as a brute and Sellar had since discharged him."[NLS DEP 313]

Shepherd, John Dryden offered some excuse for his actions.

"I agree that the timber had been cut from the horses and the animals poinded. The animals in question were trespassing and eating upon his master's grass. The people had agreed to the burning of pasture and I executed the burnings on Sellar's orders." [Richards 'Military Register and the Pursuit of Patrick Sellar']

The sheep farmers and many of their shepherds were generally people from beyond the boundaries of Sutherland, in fact beyond the boundaries of Highland custom and owed nothing to the local inhabitants; answerable only to their employers.

The Sheriff Officers, [Kenneth Murray, Alexander MacKenzie, James Fraser and Alexander Sutherland] charged with the tasks of removal were at first arrested but later sought to explain their actions.

"We acted by the orders of the said Patrick Sellar from the dread of whom at the time we durst not refuse to do anything. We knew well enough that we were doing wrong and that we had never seen the like done before.

That it was contrary to what our own free will would ever have determined and was done solely out of the dread of the said Patrick Sellar's authority. We understood that unlimited obedience must be paid in the county to the mandate and command of a factor.

We were armed with hatchets some of which had been delivered by the people from fear of Sellar We wrought more like negroes than reasonable men None of us durst venture to speak to him for fear of his displeasure and getting an answer from him as he was in such a passion Moreover, Sellar briefed them to perjure themselves." [National Archives of Scotland SRO CS 232]

The populace of Strathnaver had long been considered guilty of failing to grasp the opportunities of 'improvement' so kindly and generously being offered to them. Clinging to an outmoded and desolate way of life was how they were perceived while the people themselves desperately searched for any means of delaying and ultimately preserving their way of life.

Patrick Sellar was convinced that the people were simply guilty of being unfit for 'society' and their prolonged presence was further impeding the spread of civilisation.

"I cant keep my stores in that remote country among highland tenants, cant bring my flocks down to clip among such people. I can get no decent south country man to live among them – nor can I afford his meal costs, cows, wages

and interest on buildings, unless he herd, as well as keep stores. I can't keep sheep on Torresdale while you keep Highlanders at Invernaver." [STAFFORDSHIRE D593/K/1/3/9]

He further expanded on their guilt by association of simply being who they were and that the 'improvements' could only be to their advantage.

"It surely was a most benevolent action to put these barbarous hordes into a position where they could associate together, educate their children and advance in civilisation." [Richards 'Patrick Sellar and the Highland Clearances']

Sellar had often and previously identified their kind. Having at first praised the industry of those in Kildonan, when they then in 1813 refused to move of their land he proclaimed them.

"Such a set of savages is not to be found in the wilds of America, and you may believe their conduct is not much disapproved of by many who ought to know better." [Patrick Sellar]

Sellar obviously felt that the neighbouring estates were much less civilized and more suitable as residences for those cleared from Strathnaver. After he carried out his 1819 removals he declared that –

"Skibo and Caithness are two receptacles which had unloaded you a great deal of trash, of which you are well rid." [STAFFORDSHIRE D593]

A neighbouring Caithness landowner, Sinclair of Freswick, was in no mood to accept Strathnaver cast outs as he was also in no doubt that they were best left as 'savages'.

"Educating the people was the worst thing done in any country, for it made them know their rights. I would send for the shepherd to shave the lice of my head – the peasants were a nuisance."

He then promptly removed eighty families from Dunbeath to make room for sheep.

One of the main charges levelled at the citizens of Sutherland was that they spoke Gaelic. Sellar would frequently link their language to their lack of civilisation and was backed up by other 'improvers' James Loch weighed in by stating that,

"The prevalence of the Celtic tongue presents a barrier to the improvement and civilisation of the district, wherever it may prevail…Gaels were a species of deceit and idleness, by which they contracted the habits and ideas, quite incompatible with the customs of regular society and civilised life. [And] would never be satisfied until the Gaelic language and the Gaelic people would be

129

extirpated root and branch from the Sutherland estate." (quoted by Donald MacLeod from Loch's speeches)

However despite this apparent intransigence for change the proceedings seemingly met with their approval. Sellar in writing to the Marchioness obviously felt it wise to inform her Ladyship that:

> *"All the people of Strathnaver so far as I can learn are well pleased with what is proposed for them." [NLS DEP 313]*

William Young, chief factor, also reported to the Marchioness that all was well and going according to plan.

> *"We were all peace and quiet at the set on Wednesday and the Strathnaver men who were disposed from the Lot which Mr Sellar gets, seemed satisfied as far as I could discover, not only as he promised to accommodate a good many of them for three years but in the meantime as I mark off lots in the lower end of the Strath where certainly their children if not themselves will soon take to fishing."* [Adam]

A year later having begun his evictions Sellar was again writing to the Marchioness encouraging her to believe that the inhabitants of Strathnaver were in fact equally keen to root out those among them who were of dubious character.

Sellar to Marchioness – February 1815 …At this meeting in January a very curious story was told me of a tinker or gypsy who some years ago had intruded himself into Strathnaver, had carried from the Strathnaver a woman of that country to midst of the morass, had taken up his residence there had brought cattle and horses to it nobody knew how and was suspected of stealing sheep and cattle from all his neighbours…The people in short agreed that I must turn him out from the ground they were to possess On my arriving in Strathnaver at Whitsunday I sent notice to this tinker to be off. And the last thing I directed the constables do was to see that he was off. They went there on a Monday morning and by the time I passed in the middle of the day a crowd of the tenants and the officers had removed all his stuff into a small hut and were unroofing and demolishing his houses. I told the fellow he must quit the country otherwise I should have him taken up, and with regard to the woman who lived with him, the people agreed, as I understood to take her into the Strath a build a hut for her. [Adam]

Despite Sellar's positive claims, ultimately the people of Strathnaver refused to obey the letter of the law.

"Peaceable possession was expected but the people would not obey the sheriff's order and I was obliged to apply for a precept of ejection." [Patrick Sellar]

The Rev David MacKenzie, their Minister disagreed with Sellar's assessment of his parishioners when he presented his view to the Poor Law Commission.

> "The people are temperate in their habits and I consider them active and industrious, provided they get employment, but there is very little work for them in the parish. I remember very well the change which took place in removing the small tenants from the interior to the sea shore. In my opinion the people have been decidedly the losers by the change. They cannot command the same amount of the comforts of life as they did formerly. Their condition has been deteriorated both in food and in clothing They used to keep many cattle and they had an excellent supply of milk and of butcher meat. They likewise manufactured their own clothing and they were far better supplied with bedding and clothing than they are now." [Poor Law Commission 1834]

And, in a letter to James Loch he finally found them to be the injured party

> "In my humble opinion, the great population of Strathnaver and Strathrathy by their being removed to the shore of this parish will never have their circumstances ameliorated by the natural productions of the sea and land, so as to put them beyond the reach of the calamities they have lately suffered and which may yet recur." [STAFFORSHIRE D593/K/1/3/6]

The Times was later to describe this new homeland.

"I can describe the face of the hill where the people are placed as resembling nothing as much as a vast stone quarry; in fact it is nearly all stones which in many cases is purely moss between the rocks." [Times]

The people of Sutherland were then at the disposal of the Duke and Duchess. Even their matrimonial rights were challenged. George Fraser who served for 24 years in the 7th Highlanders complained that –

"The late Duke put an interdict on marriage. "I got my daughter married and having allowed her and her husband to dwell with me, I was fined ten shillings yearly by the factor for the offence of countenancing my daughter's marriage."

When it came to the trial of Patrick Sellar, a few of Strathnaver's disposed were called to give evidence but here too they were effectively dismissed as unworthy and they ended being portrayed as the guilty rather than the victims.

William Chisholm's story was key to the case against Sellar, for here lay the seat of the accusation.

"Sellar came to my home in June 1814 with 20 men and four Sheriff Officers, who pulled down and set fire to the house and its barns. My mother-in-law, Margaret Mackay was still in the house when it was set on fire – she was 100

years old and bed ridden. Sellar ordered the house to be fired. My sister in law arrived and carried the old women from the blazing building with the blankets in which she was wrapped on fire." [Robertson]

Chisholm went on to claim that,

"Sellar had given him 3 shillings for his timber after it had been burned (this was claimed to be by custom) but that three pound notes had also been lost in the fire."[Robertson]

Chisholm's wife, Margaret MacKay's evidence was also presented in court.

"I was away from home and returned to see smoke and her children meeting me to tell her that my mother was safe. They had placed her in a small byre without a door and a partial roof, where she was to die five days later. She gave her mother's age as 92." [Robertson]

William Chisholm's, and Henrietta MacKay's explanations as to where the £3 was kept differed and along with other apparent discrepancies in their evidence, was seized on by the defence as proof of their untrustworthiness.

Donald MacKay of Rhiloisk was cited in the indictment as saying,

"I fell prey to the fury of the assailants, became ill and was laid down for four or five days and fed by the people from across the strath until I recovered and was able to crawl to the shepherd Draper's house, but was turned away without mercy." [Richards 'Military Register and the Pursuit of Patrick Sellar']

Much later Donald MacLeod, a witness of the Strathnaver clearances in his subsequent writings sought to corroborate the evidence submitted by William Chisholm.

"I was present at the pulling down and burning of the house of William Chisholm, Badinloskin, in which was lying his wife's mother, an old bed ridden woman of nearly 100 years of age, non of the family being present" "I informed the persons about to set fire to the house of the circumstance, and prevailed on them to wait till Mr Sellar came. On his arrival I told him of the poor old woman being in a condition unfit for removal. He replied "Damn her, the old witch, she has lived too long; let her burn." [Macleod]

Donald MacLeod went on to catalogue such injustices for the people of Strathnaver as having their land and your property lifted from under them, but without any recourse to the laws of the land.

"The houses had all been built, not by the landlord as in the low country, but by the tenants themselves or by their ancestors and consequently were their property by right if not by law." [Macleod, 'Gloomy Memories']

Dignity has been described by later writers, as not having to take your clothes off in public. MacLeod highlights the indignity suffered during the removals.

> *"John MacKay's wife, Ravigill, in attempting to pull down her house in the absence of her husband, to preserve the timber, fell through the roof. She was in consequence taken with premature labour and in that state was exposed to the open air and the view of the by-standers." [Macleod]*

Others had to wait many years to provide their eyewitness accounts.

Years after Patrick Sellar had departed this earth and the next generation of the Dukedom was in place, the Government set up in 1883 the 'Royal Commission of Inquiry into the Condition of Crofters and Cottars in the Highlands and Islands' under the chairmanship of Lord Napier. Traveling throughout the Highlands and Islands they successfully captured the experiences of the like of Angus Mackay, from Strathy Point, who had been eleven years old when cleared from Strathnaver. His evidence to the Commission has all the truth of a long remembered story.

> *"My father and my mother and my brother went away that day, having got notice that if anything was upon the ground at twelve o'clock, they would be*

fined. They rose in the morning and went away with cattle, sheep, a horse, two mares and two foals, to the place they were to live in after and left me and my brothers who were younger sleeping in the bed. And there was a woman came in and said "Wont you wake up? Sellar is burning at a place called Rhistog. Many houses were burned"

"You would have pitied the people – tumbling on the ground and greeting and tearing the ground with their hands. Any soft minded person would have pitied them.

"I cannot say what was the cause, but this is my opinion. Sellar was factor, Roy was clerk and William Young was head factor and they had Lady Stafford under their control and the factors were something troubled gathering their rent. And they just blindfolded Lady Stafford and said "we will give you £100 or £200 out of that and move the people out of the place and give the money to you all at once" and the people were removed.

"After the people were removed Sellar got the place but in five years time we had a second removal and Sellar got that place as well.

"We had to move to the place called Wood of Skaill, which was an uncultivated piece of ground. It was a place that had never been laboured before. My father had to build his house with feal and no stone at all. He got no assistance from the proprietors and no compensation for the old house. He was five years in this new place when he got the second removal to Strathy Point, to the worst place in the district."

Chapter 7

THE LEGACY

Was the Sutherland Experiment for the common good? - the passage of time would prove its success or otherwise. By 1872 in a paper presented to the Gaelic Society of Inverness, its Treasurer, John MacDonald, remained unconvinced.

> *"In justification of the evictions we are continually reminded that the Highlanders have always been benefited and improved in circumstances when removed from the scenes of their childhood. Wherever such instances occur everything is made of them to prove the utility of the clearances; but not a word do we ever hear of the thousands of cases of individual and family suffering caused."* *[Transactions of the Gaelic Society of Inverness]*

In 1919 the Report of the Committee on Deer Forests came to a conclusive and thoughtful conclusion.

> *"In the cold light of history it is clear that the power of wholesale eviction by private persons was one which ought never to have been permitted."* *[Report of the Committee on Deer Forests, 1919]*

The Sutherland experiment, like all experiments, had to accommodate change if success was to be achieved.

The problem here was that those driving the change sought to do so to enhance their position. The original inhabitants of Strathnaver and the many other clearances throughout the Highlands were simply the pawns of change. Hugh Miller's assessment on the Sutherland experiment suggests that all was not a success.

> *"The Sutherland policies were, he observed, the result of the infatuation with certain doctrines which had taken hold of the Countess of Sutherland and her English husband and lowland factors. Their legendary English wealth had allowed them to use the vast Sutherland estate for 'an interesting experiment ... as if they had resolved on dissecting a dog alive for the benefit of science'. This appalling experiment had been accomplished beyond their eyes, having been entrusted to their 'footmen'. The country had been improved into a desert and its inhabitants had become a melancholy and dejected people. The shores of Sutherland are covered with what seems one vast struggling village, inhabited by an impoverished and ruined people." [Miller]*

By the time that the displacement of people for sheep was largely completed the sheep were becoming increasingly unprofitable. Andrew Matheson in his direct attack on 'greedy' landlords points to one of the basic reasons for failure – a failure that the original inhabitants would never have experienced. While they knew shortage and poverty, they knew the importance of a mixed agriculture.

> *"The rent of Ribigill run in 1817 was £1100 and in 1850 it was £700. Positive proof that rearing sheep with natural grass alone, without aid of the crops of agriculture is a sure decrease of the rent." [Matheson]*

The aim of the Sutherland 'experiment' was to make money. Sheep were favoured over people for profit and even though in the longer term sheep proved financially unviable, the cost in terms of suffering was not included in the final balance sheets.

The 'loyal tenants' of the Parish of Farr did not see it the same way. The conditions that were to improve their life and habits were so far removed from being achieved that these tenants were in such straits by February 1816 that they raised a petition, which incidentally was certified by their minister the Rev. MacKenzie.

> *"We are in a distressed and ruinous condition brought on by the fall in prices. Each increase of rent under a succession of Factors. At one time we were able to pay – without the smallest tincture of grudge- but repeated increases have become unbearable and were made worse because tenants being collected and crowded together which rendered every circumstance of life disagreeable. Now our cattle prices have halved, almost overnight. We have also suffered the*

consequence of unsympathetic landlord initiated improvements which simply added to our congestion."

Exonerated, Patrick Sellar went on to prosper. Initially he returned to the job in hand, albeit with a warning from James Loch.

" Let your orders be given directly and distinctly in firm but moderate language, without taunt or joke and whenever you can, let them be in writing which will avoid any danger of mistake which is particularly desirable where two languages are in use." [Adam]

Despite all that had gone before, further Strathnaver clearances were instigated on Sellar's sheep farm. By now Sellar has ceased to be employed by the Sutherland Estate but his successor Francis Suther charged under Sellar's lease to carry out the removals, seems to have learned nothing. Loch was furious on hearing that he had used 'burnings' in Strathnaver in the 1819 evictions.

"Depend on it no one shall ever hear of this but yourself and even you never again. I trust no acts of cruelty have been committed they cannot be passed over if they have and the punishment of them will be a triumph to the Highlanders and make the next years movings more difficult. "I wish to God you had only asked my opinion on the subject. In point of fact the impression is as bad as in Sellar's time." [STAFFORDSHIRE D593]

Sellar's Sutherland sheep farms and the inheritance of his father's property at Westfield in Moray provided him with sufficient capital to buy,

> *"...a small place in Argyllshire adjoining to steam navigation and so calculated... to prepare my Sutherland sheep for the Glasgow and Lancashire markets."*

Sellar's financial and farming prowess meant his family inherited a respectable sum however the legacy of his actions and the continuing suspicion surrounding his trial, left his family having to be alert to sporadic waves of criticism.

On the death of Patrick Sellar, a number of newspapers published glowing epitaphs. Shortly after his death, the following letter appeared in the Northern Ensign.

> *"Sir, I see a warm eulogism on the now deceased Mr P Sellar in the Inverness Courier and no doubt it is a good tribute on the part of the editor. In a soft and palmy tone he tells you that this man fancied the farm of Culmaillie; but why does he not follow him to Strathnaver? That country, meant by providence for the use of man and once occupied by the elite of Clan MacKay, in circumstances of comfort and independence, was cruelly laid waste by the departerd friend of the Courier; and although I old the old maxim 'de mortis*

nihil nisi bunum' to be a good one it is impossible for a man with Highland blood in his veins, with devoted attachment to the country and with a knowledge of the painful changes so recklessly affected in the social condition of that and neighbouring districts, not to differ with the souch of the Courier, cautious though it be. I do not deny the talent of Mr Sellar. He certainly led the way to an improved system of sheep breeding; but his talents were ever and anon employed in gratifying an inordinate selfishness, which was fed, unhappily from the moment he planted his foot on the devoted soil of Sutherland. In contriving these things, he certainly displayed great talent, and his talents produced good results for himself; but his large fortune has been acquired by means never to be forgotten by the descendents of those who suffered by his policy, whether those be now on the face of broad Scotland or in the wilds of Canada." [Northern Ensign]

The Sutherland dynasty continues.

But maybe, what Patrick Sellar, the Countess and all, are really guilty of was not stealing the land from the people but stealing the people's identity.

The inhabitants on the land owned by the Countess of Sutherland had lived according their chosen ways. Never mind that they were often hungry and destitute – they knew who they were. The Sutherland Clearances were as much about trying to create a new

143

identity for the people, firstly by abusing and denigrating their standards and way of life and then by uprooting them from the place that was an integral part of that identity. The people in the straths of Sutherland had, in the eyes of the new order, the wrong identity and as such did not fit in with their prevalent social order.

The people are gone, but certainly not forgotten. The trial of Patrick Sellar and the events around it are engrained into the heart and soul of the people. Like many lost societies, their memories are best kept in the songs, the poems and the stories -there to haunt the guilty, forever.

Bonnie Strathnaver

Bonnie Strathnaver, Sutherland's pride
Loud is the baa of the sheep on thy side
But this song, and the dance and the pipes are no more
And gone the brave clansmen that trod the green floor"
[Transactions]

Aoir air Padraig Sellar (Satire on Patrick Sellar)

Ho the black rogue, he the black rogue
Ho the black rogue, who raised the land rent.
I saw a dream
And I would not mind seeing it again;

If I were to see it while awake
It would make me merry all day
A big fire was ready
And Roy was right in it's middle
Young was incarcerated
And there was iron about Sellar's bones

Sellar is in Culmailly
left there like a wolf catching
and oppressing everything
that comes within his range
His nose is like an iron plough share
or the tooth of the long beaked porpoise
he has a grey head like a seal
and his lower abdomen resembles that of a male ass

His long neck is like that of a crane
and his face has no appearance of gentleness
his long sharp-shinned legs
resemble ropes of large sea tangle
What a pity that you were not in prison
for years, existing on bread and water
with a hard shackle of iron
strong and immovable about your thigh
If I could get at you on an open field

with people tying you down
I would pull with my fists
three inches of flesh out of your lungs
You yourself and your party
went up the braes of Rosal
and you set fire to your brother's house
and so it burned to ashes

When death comes upon you
you will not be placed in the ground
but your dung like carcass will be spread
like manure on a field's surface
Sellar and Roy
were guided by the very Devil
when they commanded that the compass
and the chain be set to measure the land

The Simpson man behaved like a dog
as befitted the nature of a seaman
wearing a blue jacket from a shop
and trousers of thin cloth
It was the black packet of the oil
that brought them to this land
but they will yet be seen drowned
and thrown up on seaweed on the Banff shore. [Celtic Culture]

146

An Old Strathnaver Man's Ballad

When I was a young, a thoughtless lad,
Along the banks of the Naver
Soldiering was then the trade
That got us land and favour
Come Angus, come Ronald, come Iver and Donald
No men on earth are braver;
If you but list, the lands then, trust,
Are your's said Factor Shaver

It was our fate to take the bait
Laid out by Factor Shaver;
With coats of red, to fire and blood,
We sped from Shin and Naver
Yes, Angus and Ronald, and Iver and Donald,
To Ireland went to save her;
The croppies fled, with wounds and dread
No corps than ours was braver
When peace came round, our lands we found,
By Donnan, Shin and Naver;
Where out forebears, for thousand years,
Had crops and flocks and favour
Then Angus and Ronald and Iver and Donald,
Had mutton and beef of flavour,

Had sheep and wool and pantries full,
And dainties sweet of savour

But soon, alas it came to pass
That sheep got high in favour;
The lady grand that claimed our land
Was led by Factor Slave-her
When Angus and Ronald and Iver and Donald
Who'd fight and die to save her,
In sad dismay, were forced away
From Donnan, Shin and Naver

This, then, the promise of land
Was broke by Factor Shaver;
His rude command non could withstand
Or plans, his wealth to favour
Though Andus and Ronald and Iver and Donald,
Might say the lands of Naver
Were their's deserved as long preserved
By their forefathers' valour
Theories, ready to dupe our lady,
Were broached by Factor Clave-her
To his command she did attend
To heartless plans he drave her
Poor Angus and Ronald and Iver and Donald

Distressed, perplexed, did waver;
While Factor Greed, with reckless speed,
Seized on the best of Naver

Factor Vaults, with jezebel faults
Has never lost her favour
Nor Factor Lake, who wrote and spake
That sour of sweet did savour
While Andus and Ronald and Iver and Donald
The men the lands that gave her,
Must now give place to suthron race,
Nor better yet nor braver

Far worse than Egypt's wasting plagues,
Wrought dismal desolation,
Glens, straths – yes parishes at once –
Were swept of population
Yet Angus and Ronald and Iver and Donald,
Thus brought to faint starvation

Were told that now, without a plough
There state was exaltation
The Factors crammed them on hard moors,
Unfit for fir plantation
Where neither sheep, nor hen, could keep

149

Itself from bleak starvation

Where Angus and Ronald and Iver and Donald

Sunk deep in degredation

(To Highland race, a foul disgrace)

As paupers on the nation

Yet finest land is left to stand

Quite in a state of nature

Without a dyke, or drain or plough

Or trace of human creature

While Angus and Ronald and Iver and Donald

Men of strength and staure

Are languishing without a plough

On moors of grimest feature

Twenty thousand 'long the shores

'Mongst the rocks and moors are starving

Without a prospect any more

To rise to their deserving

While trampled o'er they're by the score

Who all the power reserving

Of hoarding princely wealth in store

As clear to all observing

Some went down to Glasgow town

Got on, though some are weavers

But suiting best, the more went west

To chase the elks and beavers

Where Angus and Ronald and Iver and Donald

Who did their best endeavour

Got to their feet, with crops of wheat,

Far off from Factor Shaver

Alasdair G. McKayIP Editor: Scottish Heritage in New Scotland (Nova Scotia)
http://www.chebucto.ns.ca/Heritage/FSCNS/Scots_NS/Hty_Sct/High_Ch/Mem/Clr_Strathnaver.
html
 [preserved in Prince Edward Island] [Tenants and Landlords]

Bibliography

Patrick Sellar and the Highland Clearances have been analysed by many eminent writers and historians. Their works are both fully researched and cogent. There exists a number of well preserved primary resources that are available for public examination, many with willing and experienced archivists able to help bring them to light. For those seeking to validate this work and as a means of expanding their knowledge, the following list is openly accessible.

I must however make special mention of those at:

National Archives of Scotland
National Library of Scotland
Staffordshire Record Office

Sources:

ADAM, R J (ed.) (1972) *Papers on the Sutherland Estate Management 1802 - 1816,* Edinburgh: Scottish History Society

BURGHLEY, Feltham (1860) *The Sutherland Clearance: a ballad,* *Glasgow*[3]

CRAIG, David (1997) *On the Crofters Trail: in search of the Clearance Highlanders,* London: Pimlico

DISRUPTION Worthies of the Highlands [Rev David Mackenzie]: A Memorial of 1843, (1886) Edinburgh: John Grant

FAIRHURST, Horace *The Survey for the Sutherland Clearances 1813 – 1820 IN* Scottish Studies Vol. 8, 1964

FRASER, G.M. (2005) *Patrick Sellar: as a young man (1801-1810),* Librario Publishing

GASKELL, Philip (1980) *Morvern Transformed: a Highland parish in the nineteenth century*, Cambridge, Cambridge University Press

GRANT, Margaret Wilson (1991) *Golspie's Story,* Golspie, The Northern Times

GRAY, Malcolm (1957) *The Highland Economy: 1750 -1850,* Edinburgh: Oliver & Boyd

---

[3] Feltham Burghley is reputed to be a pseudonym for the poet C.A. Ward

GRIMBLE, Ian (1962), *The Trial of Patrick Sellar*, Edinburgh, Saltire Society.

GUNN, NEIL (1977) *Butcher's Broom*, Souvenir Press.

INVERNESS *JOURNAL & NORTHERN ADVERTISER*

INVERNESS *COURIER*

LOCH, James (1820) *An Account of the Improvements of the Estates of the Marquess of Stafford in the Counties of Stafford, Salop and on the Estate of Sutherland*, London

MCGRATH, John (1981) *The Cheviot, The Stag and the Black, Black Oil*, London, Methuen

MACKAY, Angus (1904) *The Book of MacKay*, Edinburgh

MACKAY, W Alex [ND] *The Achness Mission in Strathnaver* IN *MacKay Institutional Memory Papers*, Strathnaver Museum

MACKENZIE, Alexander (1994) *History of the Highland Clearances*, Edinburgh: Mercat Press

MACKENZIE, A W (1883) *The Trial of Patrick Sellar, factor on the Sutherland Estates (from 1810 to 1818) for Culpable Homocide, Real Injury and Oppression,* Inverness

MACLEOD, Donald (1996) *Gloomy Memories: the Highland Clearances of Strathnaver,* Bettyhill: Strathnaver Museum,

MATHESON, Andrew (1993) *The British Looking Glass,* Latheronwheel, Laidhay Preservation Trust

MEEK, Donald E. (ed.) (1995), *Tuath is tighearna: Tenants and Landlords,* Edinburgh, Scottish Academic Press.

The MILITARY Register (available in The National Library of Scotland)

MILLER, Hugh (1843) *Sutherland as it is and was, or How a Country may be ruined,* Edinburgh

NAPIER (1884) *Royal Commission of Inquiry into the Condition of Crofters and Cottars in the Highlands and Islands*

NATIONAL ARCHIVES of SCOTLAND

NATIONAL LIBRARY of SCOTLAND, Sutherland Collection DEP 313

NEW Statistical Account of Scotland (1835 -45), Edinburgh

NORTHERN Ensign

PATON, David (2006) *The Clergy and the Clearances,* Edinburgh, John Donald

PREBBLE, John (1969) *The Highland Clearances,* London: Penguin

RICHARDS, Eric (2007) *Debating the Highland Clearances, Edinburgh, Edinburgh University Press*

RICHARDS, Eric (2000) *The Highland Clearances: people, landlords and rural turmoil,* Edinburgh, Birlinn

RICHARDS, Eric (1985) *A History of the Highland Clearances,* 2 vols. London: Croom Helm

RICHARDS, Eric (1973) *The Leviathan of Wealth: the Sutherland fortune in the Industrial Revolution,* London: Routledge

RICHARDS, Eric (1971) *The Mind of Patrick Sellar (1780-1851)* IN Scottish Studies, n° 15

RICHARDS, Eric (1996) *The Military Register and the Pursuit of Patrick Sellar* IN Scottish Economic & Social History, 16

RICHARDS, Eric (1999) *Patrick Sellar and the Highland Clearances: homicide, eviction and the price of progress,* Edinburgh, Polygon

RICHARDS, Eric (1999) *Patrick Sellar and his World*

RICHARDSON, Dorothy (1999) *Curse of Patrick Sellar,* Stockbridge: Longstock Books

ROBERTSON, P (1816) *The trial of Patrick Sellar, factor on the Sutherland estates (from 1810 to 1818), for culpable homicide, real injury, and oppression, before the Circuit Court of Justiciary, at Inverness, on the 23rd of April, 1816, as originally prepared [1816] by Mr. Sellar's junior counsel,* Edinburgh

ROSIE, George (1981) *Hugh Miller: Outrage and Order,* Edinburgh

ROYAL Commission of Inquiry into the Condition of Crofters and Cottars in the Highlands and Islands (Napier), 1883

SAGE, Donald (1889) *Memorabilia Domestica: or parish life in the North of Scotland* Wick: W. Rae

SCOTTISH Gaelic Poetry *IN Celtic culture: a historical encyclopedia, Volumes 1-5 By John T. Koch*

SELLAR, E. M. (1895) *Recollections and Impressions*, Edinburgh

SELLAR, Patrick, Statement, 1826

SELLAR, Thomas (1883) *The Sutherland Eviction of 1814*, London

SISMONI, Simonde de (1815) Political Economy, London

SMITH, Iain Crichton (1987) *Consider the Lilies*, Edinburgh

STAFFORDSHIRE RECORD OFFICE *Sutherland Collection D593*

STEWART, David (1822) *Sketches of the Character, Manners and Present State of the Highlanders of Scotland* Edinburgh: Constable

STOWE, Mrs. Harriet Beecher (1854) *Sunny Memories of Foreign Lands*, Sampson, Low

TRANSACTIONS of the Gaelic Society of Inverness, March 14, 1872